The Generouſ Life

Steve,

Thank you so much for your
leadership and willingness to grow.
I pray this book will challenge
you toward a life of Generosity

The Generous Life

by Vince Miller

Consumed Publishing

Consumed Publishing

An extension of Consumed Ministries
Bloomington, MN 55420
www.consumedministries.com

Consumed Ministries exists to share, both in words and actions, that
Jesus Christ desires to give life to the full. We highly value our
relationships with God & people, believing through the context of
relationships we can provide the resources, speaking opportunities, and
training to effectively lead people into the abundant life Jesus promised.

Edited by Paul Wonders
Interior Design and Layout by Gretchen Miller
Cover Design and Layout by Eric Beavers
Cover image provided by Jeffrey Coolidge / Photodisc / Getty Images

Published in Bloomington, MN by Consumed Publishing
Printed by Book Printing Revolution
Minneapolis, MN

ISBN: 978-0-9766555-8-9

Library of Congress Control Number: 2011934828

Printed in the United States of America

Dedication

To my wife, Christina, who journeyed this road with me.

And to my Grandfather, Walter Lee Baker,
*   whose generosity goes beyond words.*

Table of Contents

Introduction

"I wish I could be more generous!" This is a common refrain
—and a grand copout. Few people who admit their own lack of
generosity understand that the solution is more discipline, not more
resources. A key conjunction in their statement hints at the truth of
their perspective. They might say, for example, "I wish I could be
more generous, **but...**" or, "I would be more generous **if...**" These
simple conjunctions lead to a series of excuses. Perhaps they have
incurred astronomical debt from years of poor choices. Perhaps they
just don't make enough money. Generosity must wait until they enter
a hypothetical dream situation. "Once I win the lottery..." they
might say, followed by an impromptu rendition of "If I Had a
Million Dollars."

I have someone specific in mind as I describe the selfish excuse-
maker: myself. During a twelve-year period of my life, I made this
statement over and over again. I always assumed a day would come
in which I would be called out of the monotony of living month to
month financially and suddenly catapulted into a generous stage of
life. That day never came. I prayed for that day. I waited for that day.
And I hoped that everything about my situation would change, and
then at that point I would become generous. But I found that it was
not my situation that God wanted to change–it was me.

Over the last few years I have been on a journey in understanding
the concept of generosity. Along the way I have studied finance
books and research initiatives, contemplated lessons and sermons on
the topic, and explored the issue with friends and colleagues. I have
also looked back at financial discussions with my wife, my vocational
experiences with fundraising, and the driving dreams of my financial
future. Ultimately I have looked to God and his word for insight. I,
like many, have searched long and hard for some truth on how to

think about money. This truth is hard to come by, as we live in a world that offers many differing and contradictory perspectives. I have struggled to understand this important life topic, and I recognize that it will be an ongoing tension for the entirety of my life and yours. Among all the people I've ever known—my parents, grandparents, friends, family, coworkers, and neighbors—not one person was exempt from this struggle. Together with the attendees of the church where I work, Eagle Brook Church in the Twin Cities, we strive to uncover the biblical teachings on generosity and live accordingly.

Our church and our family, like many churches and families, are facing new challenges with generosity because of the current economic changes. These changing seasons are simply opportunities to redefine the way we think and the way we live. These opportunities should clarify our mission and identity in Christ, and they should also guide us toward diligence in the places in which we have perhaps been less disciplined. I have often wondered over the last few years if the former and long-lasting bull economy led us to become lazy and sloppy with our generosity—if perhaps we became intoxicated with the former economy and now God is choosing to re-educate us. Regardless, given the current trends, we each have an opportunity to manage our own response. Making thoughtful decisions will be important in the coming years.

Generosity itself is not a simple topic to discuss. The primary objects of generosity—time and money—are loaded concepts. Many of us know first-hand that both of these items are sources of great debate in marriage and have the power to strengthen our bond with each other or lead to its demise. Our spiritual leaders find it difficult to present discussions on these two subjects in large and small venues due to the differing and strong opinions held by their audiences. Church attendees as well are often sensitive to these subjects due to the fact that pastors and teachers often discuss them in coordination with a well-planned plug for their own church's needs. In the end, Christ knows that these two topics are the chief forerunners for idolatry. In spite of the difficulty, we have to navigate these challenging topics. We must understand these challenges and begin to learn how to live generously.

As we dig into the subject of generosity, we will discover that being generous is not a way of life that comes instinctually. We live in a world that markets to our human desires—desires that directly compete with our ability to live the generous life. We will discover a hard path of obedience and discipline that is often beyond our reach. I often reflect on the story of the rich young man in Luke 18, finding echoes in my own life of this young man's reaction to Christ's call to "sell it all and give it to the poor." As much as we can be critical of this young man for walking away, I find that in my life I am much the same. Even as I study the topic of generosity, I encounter my own selfishness and lack of willing generosity. We live in a fight between the impulse to live a selfish life and the call to live a generous life. And it is that journey that compelled me to write this book. This journey can be the most fantastic journey of your life.

Acknowledgements

I would like to deeply thank a few people who have journeyed with me on this topic over the last year. First, my wife, Christina, who has spent countless hours discussing these topics with me and together with me has been fighting the selfishness of our lives. Second, my small group for allowing me the freedom to be vulnerable in these areas and encouraging me along the way; especially Scott Brophy, Todd Cina, and Chris Koelzer. Third, Johanna Price, whose input was appreciated in writing this book, as well as Paul Wonders who has been a deep source of wisdom, and whose expertise has been a tremendous service. Also Stuart Lumpkins, Mark Wylie, Jamie Miller, Mac Threinen, Lance Anderson, and many others who have been a source of deep strength. The conversations I have had with each of you has been profound and challenging. I know you do not have this all figured out—nor do I—but we have walked and talked together on a most challenging subject and it has been most enjoyable.

"You will be enriched in every way so that you can be generous on every occasion, and through us your generosity will result in thanksgiving to God."[1]

Vince Miller

---

[1] 2 Corinthians 9:11.

The Contrast

"Don't I have the right to do what I want with my own money? Or are you envious because I am generous?"
Matthew 20:15

A Central Story

One hot Oklahoma summer about 18 years ago, I was serving in a summer ministry internship. My supervisor and I began preparing for a weeklong mission trip to Houston, Texas, in which we would be taking about fifty high school students to work with the homeless. We had never led a trip like this before, yet we felt well prepared for the opportunity.

We put the students through a training course in the weeks leading up to the trip, describing what they would encounter and how they might interact with the people they intended to serve. Since most of our students came from affluent families, part of the training was helping them to understand what to wear, how to interact, and how to serve those whose life challenges appeared on the surface to be much different from theirs.

We had developed a partnership with an existing ministry in Houston; that way we could support ongoing efforts. This partner encouraged us to bring two major resources—shoes and small bags of toiletry items—that could be given to the homeless. This act of giving would also serve as a potential conversation starter for the students. So we packed a large moving truck full of toiletry items like toothbrushes, toothpaste, ear swabs, soap, and a ton of new and gently used shoes.

When we left for the trip, everything seemed to be going smoothly, but there was one student that could not get in the spirit of the trip. Mike showed up for the trip in his most fashionable attire despite our instructions to the contrary. He wore a bright blue long-sleeved polo shirt, high-end jeans, and expensive running shoes that were selling for about $175 at the time. Even among our own group he stood out. We all noticed his blatant disregard of our training, but we didn't say much, hoping his attitude, at least, might comply to our expectations.

Everyday Mike complained. About what we were doing, where we were eating, the distance we had to drive, the smells, or the lack of showers—he had some kind of complaint about anything that was not convenient for him. It did not take long for everyone to get tired of Mike. By the third day he had alienated himself from everyone, and at this point I had him within my sights at all times. And strangely enough he had a fresh, pressed polo shirt everyday. I don't know how he managed this, when most of us were back on our first rotation of clothes.

Somewhere between the third and fourth day we gave away the last of our toiletries and shoes. We just had not expected to empty a truckful of supplies in four days, so we were left with three days' worth of unexpected free time. After some discussion, we decided to spend the next few days with the people we had met and try to get to know them at a deeper level.

This decision seemed to work for everyone but Mike. His silent protests involved hanging out by himself, talking on his phone, and showing up late to specific deadlines. By day six, I could not wait to escort Mike home. Yet there were moments where I could see hope in Mike. By the end of day six, he was actually having some conversations with a select few homeless people. However I still kept an eye on him.

At the end of day seven, we were very specific about being back at the vans by 4 p.m. Earlier that morning we had packed up and loaded the vans for the trip home, but we had allowed the students to spend the day talking with our new friends who lived under the Houston bridges.

At 4 p.m. everyone showed but Mike. I was a little irritated, but tardiness was pretty much in line with his behavior to that point. We waited patiently for about twenty minutes and still no Mike. I was becoming concerned. I left the kids with another one of the leaders and went out searching for him. The more I looked, the more concerned I became.

After about fifteen minutes of searching, I spotted him off in the distance. I sped up my pace in anger—but something stopped me. He had not caught sight of me yet and I could see he was having what appeared to be a meaningful conversation with a homeless man under a busy freeway overpass. They sat next to each other on a large fallen log in front of this man's cardboard home. Here were two people that could not have been more different on the outside. One was older and rough from life, dressed in rugged attire; Mike was considerably younger and dressed in clean, bright attire that included a bright pink polo shirt, jeans, and expensive running shoes. What a contrast.

As I watched for a while, I could see this man was actually ministering more to Mike than Mike was to him. Mike at one point reached up to his own eyes to wipe away a flood of tears. Clearly something was transpiring between them, and in this moment the man put his arm around Mike to draw him close. I chose not to interrupt this divine interaction and potentially formative moment for Mike. To this day I am unaware of the full content of what they discussed, but on the walk back Mike gave me a few pieces: something about his own life and his own loneliness had deeply connected with this homeless man's life and loneliness.

After the two embraced, I witnessed something that I will never forget; it is burned in my mind forever. As they began to close off their conversation, Mike placed his foot next to the homeless man's as if to compare the sizes of their feet. Adorning the homeless man's feet were two worn pairs of shoes that clearly did not match, and on Mike's feet were those $175 prized shoes that he had bought just prior to the trip. Mike proceeded to reach down and untie his shoes. I watched as he bared his feet for this homeless man. There was no showy display and no audience. It was a powerful act of generosity for a young man whose heart had seemed so cold and self-absorbed.

I saw this one act awaken a new side of Mike. This act of generosity, done in secret and without notice, was the finest moment of the trip.

My question is this: what makes a person like Mike—or like me for that matter—become truly generous?

Another Story

While traveling through Judea, Jesus had a number of interactions that directly and indirectly involved the topic of generosity. As tension built among his followers, Jesus addressed multiple issues head-on with some rather vivid stories that had brash applications. Undoubtedly, in these particular moments, he had their attention.

In one such moment, Jesus was conversing with a small group of his followers about their own willingness to live the generous life. Peter, one of his closer comrades, tried to establish his own willingness to "leave everything to follow"[2] Jesus. In his characteristic fashion, Jesus turned this opportunity into a teachable moment that he would use to **contrast** two very different concepts: **human giving** and **God's generosity**.

Jesus shared a story that began with a landowner. Jesus portrayed him as a powerful, wise, and wealthy man. The landowner was sharp in his business dealings, cunning in his leadership, and proactive in his plans.

This man owned a vineyard. Historically vineyards were the property of people with great wealth, and with this wealth came the responsibility of land, produce, and workers.

As the story develops, we discover the landowner had devised a cunning plan: he would hire numerous workers at strategic hours of a single workday. At five specific times (6 a.m., 9 a.m., 12 p.m., 3 p.m., and 5 p.m.) the landowner went out and employed day labor to work in his vineyard. They each agreed to a contract for a day of work, but we can see that the first set of workers agreed to a very

---

[2] Matthew 19:27.

specific contract: "He agreed to pay them a denarius for the day and sent them into his vineyard."[3] The landowner's plan was well thought out and clearly premeditated, but toward the end of the day a twist in the plan was revealed.

"When evening came, the owner of the vineyard said to his foreman, 'Call the workers and pay them their wages, beginning with the last ones hired and going on to the first.' The workers who were hired about five in the afternoon came and each received a denarius. So when those came who were hired first, they expected to receive more. But each one of them also received a denarius."[4]

The twist in this story is fantastic and to the workers it appeared almost warped. I have no idea what was flooding through the minds of the followers of Christ at this moment, but we do know what the workers in the story were thinking. Their minds were spinning:

"When [the first workers] received it, they began to grumble against the landowner. 'These who were hired last worked only one hour,' they said, 'and you have made them equal to us who have borne the burden of the work and the heat of the day.'"[5]

In this single moment we see a group of workers who were frustrated and who were experiencing a deep injustice. This was **due to the comparison** they were making between themselves and the others who came at the four other hours of the day.

I would assume that at this moment there was probably a great tension arising in the hearts of the workers and simultaneously in the hearts of Christ's followers. And at the right moment the tension was lifted with an abrupt end to the story.

"But [the landowner] answered one of them, 'I am not being unfair to you, friend. Didn't you agree to work for a denarius? Take your pay and go. I

[3] Matthew 20:2.
[4] Matthew 20:8-10.
[5] Matthew 20:11-12.

*want to give the one who was hired last the same as I gave you. Don't I have
the right to do what I want with my own money? Or are you envious because
I am generous?'''[6]*

I love that last line. Did you catch it? It is the culmination of the
story and the thrust of a single point to Peter and the other disciples.
In this moment Christ reveals to us countless truths about his
generosity and the vast contrast between our giving and his
generosity.

Defining Generoſity

Generosity itself is a fairly misunderstood word. I think the
followers above embraced a novice understanding of generosity,
which is exactly the reason Jesus told the story. When we hear the
word "generosity" often the first thing we think about is the subject
of money. Even though generosity does address the subject of
money, it will and can address resources on a broad scale and the
mutual subject of time. Both time and money are central to a
discussion about living a generous life.

But to be even more precise, **generosity is far more about our
personal heart disposition toward these two subjects than the
subjects themselves.**

This is precisely why Christ's immediate followers missed the
fuller understanding of generosity. Generosity is not about how
much time or money you give but rather your complete disposition
toward the resources of your life. **To make money and time the
object of our generosity is to miss the point of living the
generous life altogether** and to become self-absorbed in our
pursuit. This is exactly the reason for the self-substantiated comment
by Peter, "We have **left everything** to follow you! What then will
there be for us?"[7] His outlook on his own choice to follow Christ

---

[6] Matthew 20:13-15.
[7] Matthew 19:27.

reduced his generosity to a simple transaction of sorts between him and God that obviously expected something in return. This is actually not generosity at all.

As we decipher the story, we know the central character of the landowner, who represents God, has a clear purpose and mission with his generosity. Although it is easy to get distracted by the landowner's wealth, his cunning disposition, his vast power, his large workforce, and the prestige of his empire, these are only details of the great drama of his mission and purposeful generosity. It is God's generosity with the riches of eternity that is the focus and ultimate beauty of the story, and he enjoys using earthly riches to accomplish his fuller mission: to give people an opportunity to spend time now and into eternity in relationship and community with him.

Based on this story, we can define generosity as **living a God-centered way of life that leads to fulfilling God's mission with both time and money.**

Defining and Contrasting Giving

Giving is a different concept altogether. Even though with a first glance there may appear to be some similarities between giving and generosity, giving is worthy of a completely different definition. The concept of giving can be much more of a contrasting idea than something that is comparable to the act of generosity.

I would think most would agree that giving is essentially a one-time action or transaction between two people. When we think about giving, we inevitably focus on the act itself—on what 'we' have done—and even on what we hope to receive for our good deed. Contrast this idea with generosity and we can quickly see the concept of generosity is centered on God's purposes and mission and not an individual's action at all. Simply put, giving is an action and generosity is a way of life.

If this one detail is true, then we can begin to see even more contrasting ideas that flow from this single idea. Giving becomes more purposed toward self while generosity is more purposed toward God. Giving is limited in scope while generosity is limitless. Giving is momentary while generosity is committed for the long haul. Giving is an obligation while generosity is completely voluntary.

GIVING	GENEROSITY
self-focused	God-focused
limited	limitless
momentary	committed
obligatory	voluntary
have to	wants to

During our church's recent food drive, we encountered a perfect illustration of the contrast between the two ideas. We were hoping the whole church would participate, so we asked even our youngest kids to help out through a project we called Hungry For Change. We sent the kids home with piggy-bank cans and the request to collect loose change for local food shelves. These young, willing, and innocent hearts took right to the task and collected more than $10,000 worth of loose change. At the conclusion of the project, one of the parents pulled me aside and told me this story:

> My daughter, Emma, has been collecting change for the food drive, and as she was scouring the house looking for change she came across my husband's iTunes change jar. What he typically does is save his pocket change in a jar and when he has collected enough, he exchanges it for an iTunes gift card so he can download music. So Emma found this jar and asked my husband if he would like to donate it. My husband then politely explained to her that those were the coins he had been saving for something that he really wanted. Emma turned to him and said, "Dad, these coins will be feeding children!" Needless to say, he donated all of his change. And she followed his lead and emptied her own piggy bank!

This story demonstrates how we can easily be self-absorbed with "our" stuff and miss the ultimate goal of money, time, resources, and capital itself. The funny thing is that the young girl understands it, because it is just that simple. Who wouldn't want to help a needy kid? Even a child comprehends this, while we adults sometimes complicate things.

The Big Contrast

Now back to the parable about the landowner and workers. There is one fairly big contrasting idea in the story that is easy to miss. It is so obvious we could skim right past it. And it is the one contrast that if missed can cause us to miss the ultimate source of God's generosity. It is found in this one simple, final text: "'Don't I have the right to do what I want with **my own money**?'"[8]

One foremost and difficult reality we must face in this life when handing our life over to God is that we must allow him lordship over all aspects of our life. This is much easier said than done, but it is a reality all Christians must face. There is nothing here we encounter during our life that is truly "ours" and nothing that we actually possess. We may attach the pronoun "my" to objects like a car, a salary, a career, or a home, but none of these items belong to us. We have released ownership of these items to God and each one of these items belongs to him. In reality we are simply managers of the resources God allots to us—and this includes money. This is the parable's ultimate point. And this is not a new idea; it is central in our relationship with Christ. Giving God "lordship" in our life implies that we manage and God owns.

Somehow the first workers contracted for labor in the story veered from this perspective. They began the day's work with everything in perspective—at least it appears they had true motives and a clear contract. As the day moved on they began to envy the

---

[8] Matthew 20:15.

owner. I think much of this was the result of comparing and contrasting the wrong items, an act that instilled within them a misplaced sense of injustice. Of course, at the close of the story we discover there is only one owner, and it is not the workers; there is only one injustice, and it is the workers' poorly drawn conclusions.

Everyday we live in this tension between manager and owner. This conundrum is hard to escape. This challenge is what makes living the generous life difficult (but not impossible). It is this battle that makes every day new, different, and exciting. But success here is important and it requires us to live everyday at its best. Even as we apply Jesus' simple and fictional story, we have to conclude that we are the workers of the vineyard. We are the ones who must ultimately live in this tension of the story. Some days, like those workers hired in the last hour of the day, we live in a clear awareness and gratefulness for God's generosity; our only desire is to humbly manage what God has entrusted to us. And there are days we join the first of the workers in envying the owner. And when we do the latter, we compete with the ultimate purposes and mission of God's generosity. Perhaps we could add to our list one additional contrast.

GIVING	GENEROSITY
self-focused	God-focused
limited	limitless
momentary	committed
obligatory	voluntary
have to	wants to
OWNER	MANAGER

It is difficult to imagine, but I have often speculated what it would have been like to be the last laborer that was invited to work. Even though the responses of this final group of workers are not highlighted in the story, I can imagine how they might have felt.

Remember, they were the last ones chosen and the first ones paid. They received exactly what was agreed upon, but definitely would have experienced the compensation differently than the others. I presume this group might have expressed tears of joy, shouted in celebration, or perhaps stood in shock with an astounded look of awe. It is this posture God seeks from one who is willing to follow, who is receptive to his purposes, who selflessly follows, and who is on a mission with him regardless of the reward. This is why I believe generosity is a hard concept for us to understand. In discussing the subjects of generosity, we must set aside the ultimate object: ourselves.

Discussion Questions

1. Have you ever been so focused on one thing that you forgot to do something else? What was it that you forgot to do? How did this moment feel?

2. Like Mike, we all struggle from time to time with self-centeredness. How is this posture detrimental to relationships with one another and with God?

3. When you compare someone else's quantity of time or money to your own, how does this impact your relationship with that person?

4. If the money you oversee is not your possession, but God's, how does this change your outlook on money?

5. What do you find to be the most significant obstacle to a God-centered life?

The Concepts

"All the believers were together and had everything in common. They sold property and possessions to give to anyone who had need. Every day they continued to meet together in the temple courts. They broke bread in their homes and ate together with glad and sincere hearts, praising God and enjoying the favor of all the people. And the Lord added to their number daily those who were being saved."

Acts 2:43-47

My Frustration with the Tithe

"Tithe," derived from an Old Testament concept, simply refers to 10 percent of anything that has value—land, goods, possessions, cattle, produce, and the like. The tithe was a mandate under the Old Governmental Law that required people to bring to God the best and first 10 percent of their goods.

I have struggled with this concept for years. Every time I hear a pastor mention the word, I become unsettled. In an attempt to understand the tithe and uncover its meaning, I have sifted through the Old Testament teachings. What I have found does little to motivate me to give; the tithe continues to feel like a legal obligation. And when I compare these passages to the New Testament teachings, I feel justified in questioning whether the tithe is relevant to the church.

My struggles with the tithe continue to drive me back to Scripture, where I find three inconsistencies with our modern understanding of the concept. The first inconsistency I have encountered is that 10 percent was not the full obligation for an Israelite. A faithful adherent to the legal system would actually have given 23.3 percent. After a short study of the Old Law, it becomes obvious that there were three leading tithes required annually, and these quickly developed into far more than 10 percent. The three tithes were the "priest's tithe" (Leviticus 27), which was used to employ the priests in the temple; the "social tithe" (Deuteronomy 12), which was a food offering that was brought to the temple; and the "welfare tithe" (Deuteronomy 14), which was 3.3 percent annually over three years and was distributed to the poor.

The second inconsistency that stems from the first is that early followers of God were actually living under a Theocracy, or religiously controlled government. These tithes amounted to a nationally enforced tax system and not generosity. The national Jewish government used the tithes in much the same way that our government uses taxes in our society: to employ leaders, and to care for one another and the poor. While I want the government to do these things, I certainly don't consider my taxes a gift or act of generosity.

The third inconsistency is the idea that 10 percent is the minimum mandate for Christians; I have heard numerous pastors and teachers propose this very thing, yet nowhere in the New Testament is this mandated or suggested. There is not one verse in the New Testament that would transport tithing concepts from the Jewish system into the establishment of the Christian church. It is very important to understand the historical concepts on tithing, but when pastors use the concepts of the tithe as a mandate for New Testament Christians, I feel manipulated by pastoral tactics— especially since I know the New Testament discusses very different concepts when it comes to money.

Regardless of how the whole concept makes me feel, the tithe was definitely an Old Law mandate and required religious action. At minimum we need to understand the tithe so that we can understand the complete concept of generosity as we read the New Testament.

Beyond the Tithe

There are a few historical moments in the New Testament regarding the tithe that have always amazed me. In the following example, we simply become spectators and learn from the master on tithing and generosity.

As the story begins, Jesus is sitting with just a few of his closest followers in the metropolis of Jerusalem over 2,000 years ago. They have situated themselves in the temple court and are surrounded by temple busyness. Followers of God in large masses are coming and going. Crowds have formed in hubs around temple vendors to purchase animals for sacrifices, as one of the great feast celebrations is just days away. The air is buzzing with activity, laughter, and discussion as families and friends reconnect after almost a year of not seeing each other. This feast celebration is an event of epic proportions.

Within view of Jesus' small group, a long line of people is forming. Jesus' followers, situated just opposite the scene, are watching the people bring their tithe offerings to God. By this very moment, thousands have made their trek to the holy city for the annual celebration; many of them are still in line. Some have saved their tithes for an entire year in anticipation of the feast and all are eager to drop their gift into the temple treasury. One by one people drop in their tithes, some making a show of the moment and parading their wealth before the audience of spectators. But there is one who is different from the others. One who stands out in this attention-getting group—a widow.

A widow's life was definitely a hard one. Whether young or old, no first-century woman would have wanted to live without a husband. Ancient Greco-Roman society offered few occupations for women, and the ones that were available were hard and demeaning. It was a man's world, and it was he that received education, worked, and garnered influence. The women were expected to find their identity and wealth in marriage, and there only. Those who lost a husband, as this woman had, were ensured a difficult journey.

Jesus follows the path of the woman. One step after another, she makes her way in line toward the treasury. In her hand, two copper coins. The essence of her life is held in the palm of her hand. She has nothing else to give after the long journey to the city. Unlike others, she has no significant possessions, no husband, no children, and no monetary wealth—just what is gripped in her hand.

I presume that the widow is feeling discomfort in this moment, and perhaps a portion of shame along with it. As she makes her way to the temple treasury, I can see her questioning whether God could do anything meaningful with such a small gift—especially in comparison with the larger and more significant gifts of others. Then the givers ahead of her move along, and the commotion subsides; it is her time and her moment. Quietly and humbly she opens her hand and drops two coins, worth less than 1/8 of a penny each, into the treasury. After observing her, Jesus makes a cunning statement:

> *"Truly I tell you, this poor widow has put more into the treasury than all the others. They all gave out of their wealth; but she, out of her poverty, put in everything—all she had to live on.""[9]*

In just two sentences, Jesus takes a poor widow's act and **moves beyond the tithe, evolving it into something new: generosity**. He contrasts showy wealth and extravagant tithes to the seeming insignificance of the underprivileged widow. In this contrast he suggests that true beauty is not found in the capacity of the gift but in the capacity of the heart of the giver. Jesus takes a moment that seems to lack beauty and draws beauty from it, revealing the extravagant gift of a generous heart.

Most reading this text will quickly notice the details. Many will catch the comparison between the rich and the poor. Then some will see the proportional difference between the wealthy people's tithes of 10 percent and widow's tithe of 100 percent. Some will catch the contrasting image that Jesus points out. And all these details are critical to the development of the story, but to only focus on these details is to miss the heart of the story and to miss the heart of the ultimate contrast Jesus is suggesting. At the heart of the story is the beauty and significance of generosity itself. And, I would suggest, the irrelevance of the tithe. Generosity is what God is seeking from us.

---

[9] Mark 12:43-44.

In this one moment, Jesus turns the tithe upside down—or perhaps right side up. His focus is not on the percentage given, but on the giver's willingness to be generous toward God and live the generous life. Jesus makes the ultimate point that God was not looking for a minimum, but instead he was looking for a maximum. To be more precise, he was looking for **maximum willingness of the heart.**

The tithe was never intended to be the finish line, but rather the starting line. Generosity is not about how much we give, but about our whole disposition toward money itself. Tithing resultantly is only the beginning, a simple transaction that hopefully leads to the way of life we call generosity.

It makes my stomach churn when we reduce the spiritual act of generosity to a simple tithe. I have come to understand this churning and discomfort in me to be the result of a great tension. It is the tension between two very contrasting ideas: the **law of the tithe** and **the gospel of generosity.** This concept is one that has freed me from my angst, renewed my understanding, and raised the bar for me on the topic of giving. Generosity is simply a whole lot more than just 10 percent. It is not a rule of minimums but a life lived of maximums. So let's add one more line to our illustrated drawing of contrasts.

GIVING	GENEROSITY
self-focused	God-focused
limited	limitless
momentary	committed
obligatory	voluntary
have to	wants to
owner	manager
UP TO 10%	10% AND MORE

Generosity of Time

If we continue to dig at the New Testament, it continues to expand the whole concept of generosity. Immediately after Jesus' ascension we encounter the establishment of the first church. In the story of Acts we read a few early summary statements that capture again the heart of true generosity:

> *All the believers were together and had everything in common. They sold property and possessions to give to anyone who had need. Every day they continued to meet together in the temple courts. They broke bread in their homes and ate together with glad and sincere hearts, praising God and enjoying the favor of all the people. And the Lord added to their number daily those who were being saved.*[10]

I have always tried to comprehend what was happening here. It appears almost utopian in nature. But the reality was simply that generosity was running rampant. Nothing in these verses was dictated, mandated, required, or ordered. I think this type of church is hard to imagine in our culture because we simply don't invest time generously like this. We can of our own means, strength, and skill accomplish most of what was happening in this passage, but one line is nearly supernatural in American culture: "Every day they continued to meet together."

Our world is so full of busyness. Work. School. Sporting events with our children. Family visits. Projects. Vacation. And in the midst of all this we have to eat, sleep, and somehow find time to be generous at our church. Generosity of time at church is only an afterthought for most of us. Unfortunately the speed of our lifestyle competes directly with our ability to have the time to meet each other's needs and the needs of others. Fatigue drains what leftover time we do have of its opportunity. Yet our willingness to be generous with our time is indicative of our heart's disposition.

---

[10] Acts 2:43-47.

One day I was coming home from work on a cold, snowy Minnesota day. I had lots on my mind and I was carrying a stack of about 10 books into the house. When I opened the door, my daughter Faith, who was then 12, greeted me. She rarely did this, which made this encounter a little out of the ordinary. Still, I did not make much of it until she spoke these words: "Daddy, I have to tell you what happened at school today!"

Until this moment, I was simply not tuned in. My mind was spinning about other things like the books in my hands, the shoes I needed to remove, the heavy winter jacket I was wearing, and my longing to use the restroom. My own pressing desires were simply louder than the excitement of my daughter. But for some reason I, for just a moment, withheld my own desires and stood in the doorway to listen—and "gave" my daughter a few moments of my time.

To allow you to really understand what Faith was about to tell me, I have to share an account of what led to this moment. At our dinner table each evening—or at least the evenings of the week in which we don't have 3 different places to be—we share "highs and lows." The purpose of this activity is simply to hear what made our day great and what made our day not so great. I have come to look forward to these times because they give me and my wife an opportunity to see the heart behind our kids' days and give us some insight into how to develop them as leaders, as family, as friends, and as followers of Christ.

Well, numerous times over the last month Faith had shared the same "low." It was about her Junior High P.E. class. She shared that the teacher gave students about ten minutes at the beginning of each class to have a basketball contest—boys against girls. Faith, who had been playing basketball for a few years by then, found this little contest to be very frustrating. Essentially there was only one other girl of the fifteen girls in her class who was athletically wired and the other fourteen hated playing sports. Faith, who is competitive, found this moment to be her "low" for weeks. In fact, the whole month of "lows" surrounded this recurring experience. As any good father would have, I tried to coach her through the experience, but we made little progress. She actually became increasingly frustrated with her teacher who did not care that the cards were stacked against the girls and that they lost every time. Too much losing for anyone can be demeaning, and I think Faith was feeling this way.

So back to the hallway conversation. There I stood, a little distracted by the things I wanted to do, yet doing my best to listen to what Faith had to say. Over the next few seconds Faith shared about gym class.

The gym teacher at the top of the hour chose two 6th grade girls and two 7th grade boys, all who loved the game of basketball, and had a little contest between them in place of the usual all-class guy-girl competition. The entire class watched as Faith and her friend played the two older boys. As my daughter told me the story, her whole demeanor slowly swelled. She was so excited; her voice sped up with every word and her body began to tense and she culminated in this statement: "And me and my friend beat the two boys in front of the whole class!" At this she emitted a tense giggle and ran off to a room down the hall where she had been finishing some homework while watching TV.

For about another full minute, I just stood in the hall speechless. My mind first drew back to my own junior high years and similar moments of excitement and disappointment. I reflected on my own moments of great defeat and great victory. Then for the next few seconds I reflected on the beauty of just simply getting to hear this story as a father. When I was a kid, I had always wished my parents had taken more interest in my stories, as I had just done for Faith. Although I had only given a little of my time, to her this was a vast investment.

But it had been a close call. I thought to myself, "You just about missed an important moment in your daughter's life, stupid." It was this reflection that was most sobering. I stood there with books in hand, sweating in my heavy jacket, and about to pee my pants thinking to myself I almost missed one of the sweetest moments in my daughter's day, month, and perhaps year.

So I called down the hall to Faith. She responded, "Yeah, Dad?" as she peeked her head around the corner.

"I am so proud of you," I said, slowly and carefully speaking each word for emphasis. Then I said it once more: "I am so proud of you!" She gave a huge smile and replied, "Thanks Dad," and went right back to watching Sponge Bob.

I am happy to say that I did not miss this moment, but the reality is I almost did. Time is a rich commodity and just as valuable as money. And just like money, we can choose to put in a little, or we can invest it completely.

Our generosity of time can ultimately be managed in two ways. One way brings joy to life, and another way leads to scars we never forget. Many of us have scars from time poorly spent or poorly used by those around us. What God wants is for us to manage and invest our time in ways that bring glory to him. We must remember that time is one of the most precious commodities we have in this life. If we generously use our time to bless others, God can work in powerful ways. As we see in Acts, when the first believers generously invested time in one another, they encountered some of the most fantastic experiences the church has ever known. Imagine if our churches were more like this today—if church was not just a place to which we might "give a little time," but an environment where "time is generously invested."

There are a few people I think of instantly when I consider the generous investment of time. It is remarkable how short the list is. Mother Teresa, famed author Henri Nouwen, my grandfather Walter Lee Baker, and a married couple I met years ago: Leland and Judy Phillips.

Leland and Judy have served generously with their time at church for decades in a single area: kid's programming on Sunday morning for 4 and 5-year-olds. They have ministered to each of my own children, so I can personally vouch for the astounding return on their investment. I am sure they could tell you stories all day long about kids who are now in college, married, or working in the mission field. Leland and Judy simply get generosity; I consider myself a novice in comparison. They are people who live counter-culturally. They don't just come to church—they have become the church. They don't just give a little time once a week—they come for the purpose of investing their time. Their example echoes the challenge of Acts 2: **"Every day they continued to meet together** in the temple courts."

Discussion Questions

1. Do you find paying taxes to the government to be frustrating? Why or why not?

2. Have you ever thought of the tithe as a tax? How does this one idea change your view of tithing?

3. What does it mean to you when you hear Jesus say, "They all gave out of their wealth; but she, out of her poverty, put in everything—all she had to live on"?

4. Imagine that Jesus has been watching your weekly, monthly or annual giving like he watched the widow. What behaviors would he note? What kind of willingness of heart would he see?

5. How does busyness influence your generosity?

The Competitors

"Then the man who had received one bag of gold came. 'Master,' he said, 'I knew that you are a hard man, harvesting where you have not sown and gathering where you have not scattered seed. So I was afraid and went out and hid your gold in the ground. See, here is what belongs to you.'"

Matthew 25:24-25

"Then he said, 'This is what I'll do. I will tear down my barns and build bigger ones, and there I will store my surplus grain. And I'll say to myself, "You have plenty of grain laid up for many years. Take life easy; eat, drink and be merry.'"

Luke 12:18-19

The Cycle

For years I have had this unsettling feeling in my life regarding material riches. I often describe this as a feeling of being trapped in a strange prison of my own material desire. A place where there seems like little hope for escape. I know many who have been trapped in experiences where they have felt the same, and for them it was the trapping of a relationship, a job, or a financial situation. In these experiences we often use descriptive terms like "dead end" or "hopeless" to describe the experience itself. For me the word "trapped" captures the full meaning. And the strangeness about this trapping is that often I do not know **how I got there** nor **how to get out.** For over fifteen years of my spiritual journey, I continued to experience this trapping, most of the time in ignorance and stupidity. But as I continued to dig into the disciplines of my faith, I came to discover the truth about my situation and discovered that my trapping was quietly leading to my own weakened generosity. I call this trapping the fear-greed cycle. So let's describe the forces of both fear and greed, and then explore how they work together to weaken my generosity and yours.

The Emotion of Fear

Fear. "An unpleasant often strong emotion caused by anticipation or awareness of danger."[11]

When I experience fear in my life, it is usually regarding my lack of both time and money. Fear typically appears first as a small and manageable anxiety. This small anxiety, if not addressed, can become increasingly more stressful over time. It often begins for me with a

---

[11] *Merriam-Webster's Collegiate Dictionary*, 11th ed., s.v. "Fear."

realization that I am not going to be able to accomplish or afford something. And if this fear is fed by a number of other circumstances in my life, then it can quickly grow out of control and lead to worry, concern, and distrust, as well as various accompanying physical ailments like sleeplessness, muscle tension, and poor eating patterns.

Everyone has varying degrees of fear in relation to time and money. Depending on how great the perceived issue might be, some of these fears can be healthy and create appropriate levels of stress that force us to respond with needed action. For example, a little bit of stress regarding debt can motivate us to adjust our spending patterns, reduce our debt, and increase our savings or income.

However we often choose a different path. On this path we ignore the motivational stimuli and fail to take positive action; this leads to further complications. Stress compounds upon stress; fear cascades into complete apathy. This place of apathy only complicates our fears and leads to complete paralysis—and here we are trapped. The key is to ensure our human fears are not impeding our judgment or, at an even more important level, our relationship with God. On the contrary, we must keep in mind that holy fear—which preempts human fear—can be a positive force that leads us to reverence and awe of God.

I have found over the years that I am fearful of so many things, especially in regard to time and money. Most of these fears are based on a general fear of the unknown. Living in this gap of the unknown for too long will eventually generate the other issues I described above. But as soon as I climb out of that gap—as soon as my unknowns become a reality—the fear usually subsides. These fears have come from not knowing how much money we'll have at the end of the month, from not knowing how much we would make or lose on a potential investment, or from not knowing if I would find a job to make the money we needed.

In 2002, as I was working as an area director for Young Life, many of these fears became a reality for my family. Young Life is a community outreach ministry that seeks to share Christ with junior high and high school students who do not know him. We planted a branch in the southeast metro of the Twin Cities, and ministry was exceptionally good. Within a couple of years, we were experiencing a profound level of ministry success. Hundreds of kids were coming to our weekly meetings and we were looking to expand. Everything we did seemed to turn to gold; hundreds went to our camps and ski-trips, and new campuses were experiencing Young Life ministry for the first time. Being the only youth ministry in town made our work easy. There was only one thing that wasn't working: the income.

Money was slim for everyone due to September 11, 2001, and the resulting economic standstill. It took time for this economic standstill to catch up to us, but when it did, it was painful. Before we knew it, we were $18,000 in debt. It was not a small undertaking to try to raise this money plus what was needed to begin operating in the black again; therefore it was time for a radical decision. And since I was the only paid staff person, the only option to deal with the cascading deficit was to eliminate my salary.

This was a difficult time for my wife and me. We were a one-income family, and taking this type of a leave was going to be financially painful. In leaving, I would essentially be putting the ministry I loved on hold, and since I was really the only fundraising agent at the time, this looked like an impossible situation. We had two young children and my wife was pregnant with our third; it was a moment full of anxiety and fear.

It is hard to explain the fear that was present in that moment; everything was racing through our heads. Finances. Bills. Health coverage. The future. Debt. Work. Children. A child on the way. We had never experienced a moment like that before. Our fears were numerous and these often led to disagreements with each other and with God.

After arduous discussions my wife and I decided to make the move. I would take three months off and work labor on a construction team, and then evaluate the future of Young Life if money came in.

Those three months were the most difficult of our marriage, and stand as such to this day. To reach our bare minimum in income, I had to work long and physically exhausting days doing demolition work on home construction sites. Even though I was thankful for the job, I went to work early and came home late and often exhausted from the labor of the day. I usually would jump right into the shower and then head to bed. I felt like I missed three months with my wife and kids during this time, which took my fear to a new level—anger.

Fear and tensions at home were high, and fear and tensions in myself were high, too, which led to some bizarre conversations with God. One day I was driving home from work so tired, so worn out, that I had an out-loud discussion with God about the current situation in my family's life. I am not quite sure how this looked as I drove down the freeway—these were the days before speakerphones and bluetooth technology—but I really didn't care at that point. I remember ending one of those conversations with God with the complaint, "After all I have done for you, this is how you treat me!" Even after this conversation I did not feel much better—in fact I felt a little convicted and concerned that God might strike me dead on the drive home. (Which led to more fear and an intensified feeling of being trapped!)

The Desire of Greed

Greed: "a <u>selfish</u> and <u>excessive</u> desire for more of something (as money) than is needed."[12] From a spiritual perspective, greed is a

---

[12] *Merriam-Webster's Collegiate Dictionary*, 11th ed., s.v. "Greed."

self-focused desire to possess wealth for your own advantage, often at the expense of others and the exclusion of the mission of God.

Greed comes naturally to the fearful, to those who have lost focus on God, and to those who are absorbed with self. Greed is a desire related to the emotion of fear. I would love to say I am not greedy, but the reality is that I struggle with greed whenever fear is exhibited in my life. This fear drives me to take back control over my life circumstances and prompts me to hoard whatever I can. We see examples of this fear-driven greed all throughout our neighborhoods and along our streets.

In our neighborhood there are a number of people who never park in their garages. I have always found this to be strange given the harsh climate that we Minnesotans live in. Why are so many of my neighbors willing to scrape snow and ice off their windshields every winter morning? The answer is simple. The garages are already full. They simply have too much stuff.

I have one neighbor who works around his yard or home each weekend and always leaves the doors of his three-car garage open, showing the neighborhood why his three cars are relegated to the driveway. In their place is stuff—stacks and stacks of stuff. And most of his stuff is cool man-stuff—things I can appreciate. Compressors, table saws, inflatable boats, wood, refrigerators, freezers, tools, fishing poles, shop vacuums, tarps—he is the neighbor I appreciate the most when I need to borrow something. But that appreciation and admiration disappears whenever I catch him climbing over his stuff to get to his other stuff. I want to laugh, but the truth is it is not that funny. The sight is almost appalling. In that moment, I recognize that my neighbor's unsightly garage is the exhibition of greed at work.

Jesus saw the same kind of potential for greed when he told the story of the rich fool in Luke 12.

At this point in his ministry, thousands of people were following Jesus. The crowds were so big that people were practically being trampled. In the midst of this, we encounter a blurting man. He randomly appears from the crowd with a pointed question and demand of Jesus. It was not the usual request for healing, cleansing, or help; his request was rather bizarre:

"Teacher, tell my brother to divide the inheritance with me."[13]

I personally find this an odd request for a public venue. I imagine him as a younger brother being rather whiny about a private family issue. This would probably resemble the bickering you would find after most family funerals. So to this whiny and blurting man, Jesus replies, "Man, who appointed me a judge or an arbiter between you?"[14]

And then Jesus turns to the rest of the thousands of onlookers and says, "Watch out! Be on your guard against all kinds of greed; life does not consist in an abundance of possessions." In other words, he suggests we are not defined by the amount of wealth we accumulate and our identity is not dependent on earthly possessions.

And then Jesus proceeds to tell the most fascinating story about greed.

It is a story about a wealthy man who owned a large acreage of land on which he farmed grain. On a certain year, this wealthy man experienced an exceedingly large harvest. This windfall led to a concern: what to do with the extra harvest.

"This is what I'll do. I will tear down my barns and build bigger ones, and there I will store my surplus grain. And I'll say to myself, "You have plenty of grain laid up for many years. Take life easy; eat, drink and be merry."'

[13] Luke 12:13.
[14] Luke 12:14.

"But God said to him, 'You fool! This very night your life will be demanded from you. Then who will get what you have prepared for yourself?'"[15]

Jesus eloquently points out how greedy we get when we get a little "extra" in our life. I have found this to be true in my own life. When I get even small amounts of extra, my first impulses are always focused on myself. It is an expected human instinct in me. I am really not that different from the blurting man in that when I do get extra, my first impulse is to scheme what I will do with it. I rarely attempt to discover why God gave it to me and what God wants me to do with it, which would be the correct first impulse. One of the gripping parts of the story is how quickly the greed impulse kicks in for the rich fool and progresses into a selfish scheme. If you read his response carefully, you will notice twelve personal pronouns in two and a half verses (Luke 12:17-19a); that's eight I's and four mys. Notice how self-concerned this man has become, and how quickly greed has eaten at his life. This reaction is much like mine, and I would suggest we all initially respond this way.

Greed is not just a struggle for the wealthy, but for everyone who comes into moments of extra. I have found for me it is my extra that gives greed opportunity in my life. I confront my greed when given a raise, receiving an unexpected check, or getting that annual tax refund. In these moments my true and often ugly self will surface and surprise even me. This side of my human nature is often distracted by the latest gadget, the newest style, a fun excursion, an item for my home, a cool new tool, or this hot new device that for some reason I need to have. I am often privately ashamed of this impulse and have a hard time even writing about it. But the impulse, which speaks a shameful truth about my own sinful nature, is one I must face and confront.

---

[15] Luke 12:18-20.

In 1988, back in my early twenties, I was addicted to restoring antique cars. By the time I was 21 I had probably owned a dozen vehicles from the late 1950s and earlier. Some I casually fixed up, some I sold to make a little money, and some I chose to completely restore. Although I owned a few different makes of cars, I had a favorite model: early air-cooled Volkswagens. I was privileged to restore some pretty sweet vehicles during that period.

So in the summer of 1988, I was on an excursion with a friend looking for parts for a couple of our cars. These excursions were really hunting expeditions and we had been on them together dozens of times. What we would typically do is gather up about $500 to $1,000 in cash, stuff it into our pockets, and head out searching the California Valley for cars and parts. The process was simple: we just drove around hunting remote properties for deserted autos that we could either purchase or strip for parts. When we found something that caught our eye, we would stop, knock on the door, and inquire. Sounds a little hokey and a little like watching *American Pickers* on the History Channel, and it was strange at times, but we came home from every trip with something interesting.

On this particular day we were in the Napa Valley and came across an old hippie (not an unfamiliar occurrence to us given our love of Volkswagens). We met him at a highway stop after spotting his ride, a pristine 1956 VW 23-window bus. His bus was European style with front safari windows and sported a super-clean roof rack, which totally stood out on this old highway. As we started talking we quickly learned that he was an old Vietnam veteran, very intelligent, and a little toasted from his daily smoke. Talking with people like this was key in finding cars and parts, regardless of whether they were swappers, restorers, or collectors. To us it was simply business networking; the fact that we got to hear so many incredible life stories was an extra perk and made this kind of activity a total blast. This particular guy was clearly a restorer who could connect us to other resources. After a short conversation, he invited us back to his home. These invitations always made us feel a little awkward. We would feel a mix of anxiety and expectancy at the thought of going to a stranger's home. But we always felt safer going as a pair.

We followed this old hippie about fifteen minutes down the highway and then onto a rather large Napa Valley vineyard. It was somewhat of a surprise that someone with his hippie-like demeanor would live on such an upscale property, but we had met so many different types of people that stuff like this surprised us less and less. We pulled off the highway and drove a couple of miles down a long dirt access road that passed right through the middle of the vineyard. In the distance we caught a glimpse of a couple of barns on the back of the property and soon began to realize that this was where he lived—in a barn.

After pulling to a stop and hopping out of our car, it became clear to us that this was not only his home, but that he had a job on the vineyard as well. In a brief discussion with the old hippie, we discovered his job was overseeing labor on this vineyard and that he was a longtime friend of the vineyard's owner.

His home was especially fascinating. It was a well-constructed and fully insulated pole barn. Essentially he drove his bus right into his home. When he opened the barn doors, we looked into the coolest house we thought any car fanatic and bachelor could have. His house was awesome! Downstairs was an auto shop fully outfitted with every tool imaginable, and extremely clean. Upstairs he had a studio-apartment living area that overlooked the shop below, much like a large loft. The coolest part was the fireman's pole right in the middle of his living room that gave him access to his shop below. We talked with this guy for hours, hearing about his life, sharing stories about our love of cars, and discussing the best places to find parts in the area.

As we were about to leave, I inquired about his role on the vineyard and his relationship with the owner. He shared only a few details, but right when we were about to walk away he asked us if we would like to see the landowner's barn. He lifted his arm and pointed to the other and much older barn that sat about five hundred yards from where we were standing.

I thought this request was rather random. He did not allude to what was in the barn but just asked if we wanted to see it. Honestly, I thought for a moment that this was a bad scene out of an old horror film, but curiosity immediately got to us both.

We followed this guy over to a rickety old wooden barn that looked like it was built around the 1900s. It was painted red and you could tell it had been painted over multiple times. Attached to the rear of the barn were pigpens that looked like they had been unused for years. The barn itself was structurally sound but definitely rotting and you could see light peeking through long exterior boards that had been shrinking over time. The total size of the structure was about as large as a football field in length and width and close to two stories tall. The old hippie reached for the big barn doors and what was inside was the most incredible sight I had ever seen; to this day I have never seen anything like it.

Inside of this barn sat about thirty automobiles from the 1930s and 40s. High-end automobiles, including models from Bentley, BMW, Mercedes Benz, Buick, Lincoln, and Jaguar. About half of the cars were hanging from the rafters by strange chain contraptions that lifted the entire vehicle off the ground. About ten of these were convertibles, and the rest hard tops. To our astonishment, many of the cars had factory-made tires on them, completely original paint, and immaculate exteriors, and a couple barely had 100 miles on the odometer. Many of these cars had been purchased off the showroom floor and placed in this barn more than fifty years prior, and had not moved since. Clearly this landowner was a collector. We spent about an hour in this barn sitting in cars and gazing under the hoods. It was like we stepped back into the 1930s and 1940s for an hour of our lives.

The depressing part of the whole experience was that these amazing cars sat partially exposed in that old barn. Since the barn was deteriorating from years of use, it was not protecting the cars entirely from the elements. A layer of field dust about an inch thick covered the exteriors, the humidity from the vineyard air was rotting the upholstery and convertible tops, and the field mice had completely chewed through the wiring in many of the cars. Our excitement gave way to a strange form of sadness. That sadness made the joy of this hour quickly flee as we closed the doors on the old barn.

I think of this experience every time I hear the story about the rich man who wanted to build bigger barns. Our extra fades so quickly; our barns are pointless when they simply become places for our extra to rot.

Fear and Greed

In the parable, Jesus uses the visual of the bigger barns to neatly tie the fear-greed cycle together. The rich fool's fear of poverty leads him to greedily hoard his extra. I hope you see how these two concepts are so tightly intertwined. His **fear** was his insecurity about the future and he chose to use his **greed** to subdue this insecurity and manipulate it to create happiness—or what I might call a false sense of security. This man's greed led him to a pseudo-happiness, which led him to use money in a dishonorable way, thus exchanging potential generosity for greed. Isn't this so true of our lives? It only takes a little fear and a little greed to initiate this unfortunate cycle.

Sometimes this fear-greed cycle can really sneak up on me. It starts with a small comparison that I make—usually between something I have and something I don't—and then it slowly begins to develop into something more. In small doses our world finds greed to be socially acceptable, but unfortunately this small dose does not remain small. Soon this desire becomes stronger, and what you wanted becomes something you need, something you have to have. On it grows, leading to forms of covetousness and lustfulness; when you act upon these desires, the normal result is a feeling of buyer's remorse. Before you know it, greed has lured you in, deceived you, and taken you down. And even though the world may accept this behavior and even write it off as permissible, God does not.

Together, fear and greed can be a powerful force of deception and distraction. And once you get ensnared in this evil cycle, it is very difficult to escape.

My conclusion is this: **we are fearful when we don't have time and money, and greedy when we do.** And the emotions intertwined in this cycle are extraordinarily powerful. When we live in this cycle for too long, our wisdom can get muddied and our world can close in on us.

∫tuck for a Rea∫on

About a year ago I learned what it feels to be in the middle of this life-draining cycle.

My wife and I recently purchased a gently used SUV, a VW Touareg, in pristine condition. It was a car Christina really wanted as she was eager to move out of the minivan stage of life that we had lived in for the previous 10 years. We have always paid cash for our cars, and this situation was no different. We had the money saved and, even though it felt very impulsive, we bought it within ten hours of seeing it; it was the only car we looked at, but we felt the price was right.

This car was nice. Leather interior, heated seats, sunroof, and super-excellent condition. I felt a little buyer's remorse after purchasing it, but my wife felt none! And she looked sexy in it.

Well, this quickly became the poorest financial decision we had ever made. Our greed led us to discover the joys of owning a higher end car: the cost of repair and upkeep. Joy!

A number of items drove us crazy, chief among them the electronic ding that sounded for just about everything. When you did not fasten your seat belt immediately, it dinged. When it was below freezing (which was every day), it dinged. When fluids were low, it dinged. When it was time for an oil change, it dinged.

We also began to discover that purchasing items for this car was not cheap. The first thing we had to replace was a headlamp bulb, which cost $178. Next up were the windshield wiper blades that could not be found at any auto parts store but only from the manufacturer—these cost $50. The oil change alone was ridiculous —it cost $90 because you had to use five quarts of synthetic oil. And this was only the beginning!

Once things started to fail on the Touareg, we discovered that all the parts were exclusively available through the manufacturer. I guess German engineers were pretty cunning on this one.

The next thing to ding on us was the tire pressure sensor monitors (TPMS). Apparently some cars are now being built with pressure sensors in the tires that monitor the pressure of each individual tire in the car and send a signal back to the dashboard to tell you how high or low the pressure is in the tire. Cool, right? Not even a little. Because of our frigid Minnesota winters, the air temperature was constantly changing the pressure in the tires. So when I pulled into my heated garage, the pressure changed, causing the pressure sensor to ding all the time. We would constantly get a "flat tire" message on the dash. I did everything within my power to ensure the tires were inflated to suggested winter temperature settings. This did not fix the problem. For weeks I tried playing with the pressure, but at last I could see there was no possible way to repair this issue. I finally took the car in. After an hour in the VW service lobby, they decided the best course of action would be to replace all four sensors and the command module that receives the signal—this costs $500 because you cannot replace just one. Whatever! I chose not to pay this and figured we would simply ignore the issue. Well, it was easy for me to ignore since I was not driving it daily. But once it started giving my wife headaches, that meant I had a headache. So I went out and removed the fuse to the dinger—cost: $0. Ha, I thought I had them.

But it was a short-lived celebration. Over the next few months, the maintenance costs continued to pile up:

- Nail in side of tire - $200
- Three nails in two more tires (that same week) - $400
- Drive train bearing blowout - $2,200
- Misfiring spark plugs - $150
- Another oil change - $90
- Brake light sensor - $50
- Water pump & timing belt - $600

At the end of all this we were seriously broke and frustrated. We traded this car in after the last repair because we could no longer tolerate it. We owned the vehicle for just over six months, but the experience nearly wrecked our pocket book. We have been exceedingly happy with the Ford F-150 we now own. Not one repair in over seven months.

I see our Touareg experience as a parable of how we feel when we get stuck in the fear-greed cycle. We can feel beat up, confused, taken advantage of, stricken with difficult decisions, angry, frustrated, and in turmoil. A single impulsive purchase led to additional poor and fearful decisions that devoured our finances. Needless to say, this was one of the most difficult financial years we have had in a long time. Every time I see a Touareg on the road, I am reminded of those six months and how fearful we were.

There is really only one reason we get stuck in this life-sucking cycle in which the desire of greed and the emotion of fear begin to do their work. In the Gospel of Matthew, Jesus engages in a lesson that is seemingly about money but is really more about something else: the bottom-line reason we get stuck in this ominous cycle!

Jesus tells of a wealthy man who left for a journey and left three men in charge of some of his wealth. Each of the three men was given a particular amount of gold. The first was given five bags of gold; the second, two bags of gold; and the third, one bag of gold. While the wealthy man was gone, the first two doubled their wealth and the last hid his money in the ground.

When the wealthy man returned, he accounted for his wealth and rewarded the first two men for their good work. But the wealthy man grew disappointedly angry about the third man's decision to bury his gold.

> *"You wicked, lazy servant! So you knew that I harvest where I have not sown and gather where I have not scattered seed? Well then, you should have put my money on deposit with the bankers, so that when I returned I would have received it back with interest."*[16]

The wealthy man in this story is supposed to be representative of God, and he was angry for one reason alone: **mismanagement**. This parable was really not about mismanagement of money. Even though the topic of money appears to be center stage, this is not the case. The topic that is actually center stage is **God's ultimate mission** and it is this mission that the lazy servant mismanaged. Somehow the third man just simply missed the reason he was given the money in the first place. He focused too intently on the money itself, not realizing it was simply the means of accomplishing something more important.

And I believe this is the primary reason we get stuck in the fear-greed cycle. We so rarely think of our time and money and our very lives within of the context of God's mission. Yet God has given us our resources and our new life in Christ for precisely this—the management of his mission. A well-managed life requires discipline and focus; these ensure we will not fall victim to this self-absorbing cycle. (Remember that earlier definition of generosity: **a God-centered way of life that leads to fulfilling God's mission with both time and money.**) It is not about the subjects of time and

---

[16] Matthew 25:26-27.

money themselves but about living on mission with God in a way of life that leads to honoring choices with time and money.

Break the Cycle

Getting outside of this deadly cycle often requires a jolt. Simply put, a jolt of pure generosity will often set us free from this endless loop. Sometimes this jolt is receiving an act of generosity and sometimes the jolt is an internal decision to act in generosity. Let's discuss both and how they work.

First, let's explore how being the recipient of generosity can jolt us free from the fear-greed cycle. To do this, let's recall my own personal story of fear from earlier. The one where I am riding home in the car angry with God.

Well, on the way home from work at the construction site, I decided to stop by the Young Life office. Now remember, I have just had a pretty candid discussion with God. I had not been to the office in weeks, and figured it was at least time to pick up the mail and pay the bills if need be with whatever money we had in the cash account. When I got there, I made a phone call to a friend and began riffling through the mail. Most of the mail was insignificant, except for one letter that I almost tossed in the garbage. But since I was stuck at the desk anyway for the duration of the phone call, I decided to kill a few seconds and open the letter.

The letter was from a local law office. As I talked on the phone, I opened the envelope and found a formal letter neatly folded inside. I removed the letter, and a check from inside the envelope fluttered out and landed face-down on the ground.

Getting a check in the mail was not unusual for us. Sometime dozens of checks would come to the office each week from local donors, and I assumed this one was the same.

So instead of bending down to get the check, I read the letter I was holding in my hand. As I unfolded it, I noticed it was printed on fine-quality cotton paper with a beautiful watermark adorning the interior of the page. It was a very brief letter with just two lines.

> Dear Mr. Miller,
> Clients of mine wish to make an anonymous donation to Northern Dakota County Young Life. Enclosed you will find a check for $18,000 dollars.

Well, this sure was a jolt of generosity. In awe of this letter and a little shocked, I hung up the phone with my friend mid-sentence. I am pretty certain I did not say goodbye. I then reached down and picked up the check and just looked at it. And then I re-read the letter again. And again and again while looking back and forth between the letter and the check.

My first thought was who did this? But after the desire to know fleeted, my second thought was even more humbling: "Uh, God, about the conversation on the way here…" Talk about feeling stupid. I don't know if I ever told anyone about this conversation till now, not even my wife. It was just a little too humiliating.

In one swift moment, God had me right where he wanted me. In that moment, he taught me to fight fear with faith. I felt God say something like this:

> *"Do not be anxious about your life, what you will eat or drink; or about your body, what you will wear. Is not life more important than food, and the body more important than clothes? Look at the birds of the air; they do not sow or reap or store away in barns, and yet your heavenly Father feeds them. Are you not much more valuable than they? Who of you by [fearing] can add a single hour to his life?"*[17]

To this day I have no idea whose generous gift this was, but the effects of this jolt have yet to wear off. The change in my outlook has been different after this day simply because I was freed from the ominous fear-greed cycle. My wife and I found hope again, found

[17] Matthew 6:25-27.

peace again, and grew to trust God even more than before with our time and money. All this resulted from a simple act of another person's generosity that was so impeccably and supernaturally timed in my life. And all I had to do was receive it.

The second jolt is a decision to act in generosity. At Eagle Brook Church we titled our decision to act "The $20 Challenge." Very simply, the goal of the $20 Challenge was to take a single $20 bill and sit with your family, spouse, friend, or loved one and discuss where and to whom you could be generous. The only rules of the game were that you could not give it to the church, you could not expect to receive something in return, it should be done in secret, you had to make a decision together, and you had to pray about it.

I remember dreaming of what this could look like—to see hundreds, if not thousands of people engaging in the beauty of generosity.

As unremarkable as it may sound, this one challenge was revolutionary in tremendous proportions to our community but especially in the heart of our attendees—the ones sharing the generosity. This little activity taught disciplines with time and money that we don't often engage in: prayer, discussion, intentionality, selflessness, and trust of God, to name a few.

The thing I learned as we led people through this activity is that these disciplines are corrective to emotions like fear and greed. And I watched hundreds of families during these weeks share stories of joy, love, excitement, and peace that oppose the fear and the greed of this world.

Here is just one story from a woman named Cathy Seiford:

> About a week after we were given the $20 Challenge, my husband suggested during the ride in the car to church that we pick up the tab for someone at our local breakfast stop during our usual "before-church" breakfast. So on our way

there we talked with our children about picking out a family and paying for their breakfast.

We were seated in a separate area with fewer tables, so we didn't see any other people there until an elderly couple was seated in a booth near us. They were an adorable old couple, and we guessed that they could have been married for fifty or more years.

My eleven-year-old agreed that we should choose this couple. I scribbled a note on the $20 Challenge Green Card to tell them that we paid for their breakfast and to have a terrific day. I handed the note and a $20 bill to our waitress and explained the plan. She was very touched. We felt great, and we thought that was the end of the story.

Well, two weeks later that same waitress saw us at the same breakfast stop and ran over to us. She said, "I have to tell you what happened when you paid for that couple's breakfast!" She said that when she told the couple that we paid for their breakfast, the elderly woman took her hat off and revealed her shaven head. She was a cancer patient and she had been having chemo treatments since November and this was the *first time* she and her husband had gone out to eat since then. They were so moved by the gesture that someone paid for their meal. Imagine that! The prompting to pick them was for a reason! Probably the best $20 we've ever spent.

This story is one of many hundreds. Some made us laugh and others, like this one, brought a pause and a tear. But the one thing that really caught me off-guard was not the good it did for other people that received the gifts, but the jolt it gave to the people who found a way to be generous. Lives were changed on both ends of the spectrum; both parties received a jolt. For some a jolt of hope, for others a jolt of joy, for some a jolt of love, and for others a jolt of generosity straight from the heart of God.

Breaking the cycle is simple. Be generous. Generosity is the only jolt that can free us. A true and pure act of generosity is powerful enough to set us free from the bondage to this deadly life-absorbing cycle. And if it is a true act of generosity and completely lacking of selfish purposes, it can do a world of good for others and us.

Discussion Questions

1. Two things we often feel we lack in this life are money and time. Which of these do you think has the greater potential for generating a fearful attitude in you?

2. While everyone struggles with greed to some extent, consider for a moment someone who you feel is especially greedy (without naming them). This person may be an acquaintance or friend, or perhaps a celebrity. How does greed manifest itself in this person's life?

3. Have you ever fallen victim to the fear-greed cycle? In what life circumstances are you most susceptible to the influence of fear and greed?

4. Describe a moment when you have watched a friend or loved one break free of the fear-greed cycle. How did this happen for them? How has this happened for you?

5. How can you receive an act of generosity and share an act of generosity this week to get your life back on mission?

The Distractions

"When one of the Pharisees invited Jesus to have dinner with him, he went to the Pharisee's house and reclined at the table. A woman in that town who lived a sinful life learned that Jesus was eating at the Pharisee's house, so she came there with an alabaster jar of perfume."

Luke 7:36-37

Once We Escape

Once we have escaped the fear-greed cycle, the key is to stay out. Yet God will allow us to live in the fear-greed cycle if we insist on doing so. We must daily resist the pull of fear and greed, forces that continually oppose our attempts to live a Christ-centered life.

The Distraction of Self

Self-absorption or self-centeredness competes with our ability to be generous. When our focus is on self, then generosity ceases to exist and both fear and greed kick in and lead us down dangerous paths. It is no wonder that those of us in countries with lots of material wealth get distracted so easily. Let's look at a couple of examples.

We have probably all encountered a homeless person panhandling on a street corner. And most of us have spent this moment wrestling with ourselves. What do you do? Do you make eye contact or look away? Do you walk closer or take an alternate route? Do you read the handwritten sign or simply try to ignore it? Regardless of how you interact, how many times have you handed this beggar money, bought him lunch, or offered him something of substance from your own life?

I have struggled through this dilemma for years. Very few times, I must confess, have I handed a beggar money. My usual first activity is to **rationalize** why I would not give him money.

This became more complex once I had children, who in their innocence asked the obvious question, "What is that man doing, Dad?" My children's innocent questions caused me to pause, and drove a stake into my heart. I am continuing to grow in my responses to street-side beggars, and have learned that **explanation and rationalization** should not be a part of these encounters.

Some may say it is unwise to give money to a homeless man because of how he "might" spend the money. However the question I have to ask myself is why do I rationalize this in the first place? The only answer I can come up with, if I am honest, is that I by nature am self-absorbed, or self-centered, and rationalization is just a symptom of this greater problem.

C.S. Lewis's stepson Douglas, in recounting his stepfather's life, drew attention to Lewis's enormous compassion and generosity. Douglas remembered a moment where Lewis—or Jack, as he called him—and a friend were walking together to a meeting. On this particular day a beggar approached them. The beggar asked them for some spare change, whereupon Lewis emptied the entire contents of his wallet. Once the beggar had gone, his friend said, "You shouldn't have given that man all that money, Jack; he'll only spend it on drink." Lewis replied, "Well, if I'd kept it, I would have only spent it on drink."[18]

I think this short encounter speaks a powerful truth. **We spend all this time rationalizing that a beggar would waste our spare change when that is exactly our own intentions.**

This rationalization is one of our many distractions. And this distraction will almost always lead to us making a self-centered decision with our money and time. And the result is distraction from God's purpose for the money and time he gives us.

A Distraction of Biblical Proportions

In the Gospel of Luke we encounter Jesus as he was making his way to Jerusalem and the home of Mary and Martha. Along the way he stopped at a village where he took advantage of his usual opportunity to mix with local crowds.

---

[18] Liggins, Steven. "According to the Son." *Southern Cross Quarterly,* Spring 1998.

Here he encountered an expert in the Jewish law. This well-read, well-educated man was ready for a little legal sparring on a theological subject. His question was simple: "Teacher, what must I do to inherit eternal life?"[19] Possibly his question was a genuine inquiry; we really don't know, but I have always been curious about the tone and inflection of his voice.

Jesus shrewdly responded with a question of his own. "What is written in the Law?" he replied. "How do you read it?"[20]

In characteristic fashion, the lawyer answered with the most familiar Jewish text from the Old Testament: "Love the Lord your God with all your heart and with all you soul and with all your strength and with all your mind," and "Love your neighbor as yourself."[21] And to this Jesus replied, "You have answered correctly. Do this and you will live."[22]

It appeared at this point that the sparring was over, but as Jesus began to turn away, the lawyer asked one more question. This time the question has a pressing tone and inflection. The lawyer clearly intended the question to serve as a test of wisdom and wits. Perhaps the first question was too simple, but this next one would have him.

"And who is my neighbor?"[23]

This question was no small question. It was an often-debated question in Jewish circles; religious lawyers had developed some complicated legalistic parameters around this question that made an answer problematic.

Jesus told a story in reply. As with all his other parables, this story had a vivid point and a powerful application. And this particular story offered a mutual chastisement.

---

[19] Luke 10:25.
[20] Luke 10:26.
[21] Luke 10:27.
[22] Luke 10:28.
[23] Luke 10:29.

In Jesus' story a man, assumedly a Jew, was making a journey from Jerusalem to the nearby city Jericho. This was a typical route, familiar to many in Jesus' audience. It was a 3, 300-foot descent along seventeen miles of winding highway. The journey took about a day on foot. The highway was known as the "Way of Blood" due to the prevalence of highway robbers. Lone travelers were especially at risk to violent attacks. And this is exactly the scenario that Jesus described: "A man was going down from Jerusalem to Jericho, when he was attacked by robbers. They stripped him of his clothes, beat him and went away, leaving him half dead."[24]

So far the story probably made a lot of sense to the lawyer. It was a pretty true-to-life story that could have been a real occurrence. But then Jesus threw in a twist. Two people came by. The first passerby was a temple priest. He came upon the situation, viewed it, and then chose to pass by on the other side. The second was a Levite—one who served in religious duties at the temple. He, too, came upon the situation, looked at the injured man, and chose to pass by as well.

At this point in the story, all the events would have seemed credible enough, though the appearance of the priest and the Levite probably stung the lawyer a bit, given that he was of a related occupation.

There were a number of probable reasons why the priest and the Levi chose not to stop. They might have thought the robbers had left the man as a trap and were lurking nearby. They might not have had time to make the return trip to the temple that would have been necessary had they touched an unclean, bleeding, dying, or dead man. It could be they were simply lazy. The bottom line is that they, like me at times, **were distracted by all their legalistic rationalizations**. Regardless of these distractions—perfectly logical rationalizations—these two men definitely lacked generosity of both time and money.

---

[24] Luke 10:30.

Meanwhile, Jesus continued with his little story, adding in an offensive character: a Samaritan. Jews, of which the lawyer was one, and Samaritans descended from the same heritage and worshipped the same God, but a number of slight legal differences led great contentions between them. Jesus' mere mention of the Samaritan no doubt spurred the curiosity of the lawyer and caused him a little indignation

Jesus began to contrast the Samaritan's behavior with that of the priest and Levite. The Samaritan came upon the scene and stopped; the following verse says, "He took pity on him."[25] This is in complete contrast to how the first two men responded. Something must have been taking place within this Samaritan's heart. Now, the great assumption of the story is that the wounded man is a Jew. Essentially this wounded Jewish man was left abandoned and uncared for by two religious men of his own race and religion, and the one who felt compassion and pity was the one who was legally the most despised.

Jesus went on to describe the man's vast generosity. The Samaritan dismounted his mule and went to the injured man, touched him, bandaged him, and poured healing ointment on him. Then he lifted the half-dead man, brought him to the closest inn, and continued to care for him. But he didn't stop there. He not only gave of his time, but also his money; the next day he took from his own pocket two days' wages and gave it to the keeper of the inn. "Look after him," he said, "and when I return, I will reimburse you for any extra expense you may have."[26]

I am sure the crowd was a little uncomfortable with the path this conversation had taken. Jesus had cunningly confronted not only the lawyer's question, but the people's prejudices as well. And with the lawyer back on his heels, Jesus asked him, "Which of these three do

---

[25] Luke 10:33.
[26] Luke 10:35.

you think was a neighbor to the man who fell into the hands of robbers?"[27]

I doubt this question was well received. The story dictated that the only correct answer would be the Samaritan, and Jews refused to even verbalize their name. So here is the lawyer's response: "The one who had mercy on him."[28]

I am sure this was a hard line for the young lawyer to verbalize. Notice no mention of the Samaritan's race or religious affiliation— just the neutral phrase "the one." And at this Jesus concluded, "Go and do likewise." [29] Those last words, I am sure, were the ultimate slap in the face.

Essentially Jesus was saying, "Stop debating, stop theologizing, stop rationalizing, stop legalizing and start doing something. Stop letting the stuff in your head distract you from God's mission."

This is the conclusion that I have come to regarding the question of those in need around me. Sometimes the best response is not "No" but "Yes." **Sometimes I need to fight the temptation to rationalize away an opportunity to help someone, and just respond.** After all, who wants to live a life defined by a long series of noes? Not me; I want my life to be defined by something different: the "yes" of the mission of God.

More Distractions

To complicate the matter of distractions, let me share about a campaign donation my wife and I made about two years ago with a local church. This particular church was launching a capital campaign to expand ministry outreach into the community. It is not a church we attend regularly, but it is in our neighborhood and we felt it would

----

[27] Luke 10:36.
[28] Luke 10:37.
[29] Luke 10:37.

be a good opportunity to support a local church that was getting serious about evangelism.

After much prayer, we decided to donate to this campaign, pledging $5,000 over the course of the year. For us this was definitely a stretch, but we were very committed to this decision.

As we began to fulfill our giving commitment, we felt very good about the decision. But about halfway through the year it became clear that the campaign was floundering. We noticed that the vision was not being fulfilled as promised. Soon we heard rumors that the campaign might indeed fail to come to fruition for a number of reasons. Of course my wife and I were more than disappointed; we had given the gift in hopes of expanding God's kingdom and were coming to realize that our sacrifice would not have its intended effect.

After a few weeks of considering what we should do, I finally contacted the pastor. He said that the campaign was on hold due to financial difficulties with the general fund and that they intended to use some of the money raised from this campaign to back-fill the needs in the general fund. As politely as I could, I shared that we would be retracting the rest of our gift, and that he was welcome to use what we had already given toward these new needs and purposes. This was an arduous decision to make, and the pastor handled the conversation exceedingly well.

Did we make the right decision? I asked myself this question over and over, and finally determined that the answer was no.

It was undeniable that the pastor and leadership of this church had miscalculated the potential of the campaign. Perhaps the campaign was too bold. Perhaps it was the wrong timing. Perhaps financial backing was the wrong commitment to ask of attendees. But the exact reason didn't matter. A contract had been broken, and I felt justified in withdrawing the remainder of the pledge.

The unfortunate reality that my act revealed was that **my gift was not a true act of generosity, but an obligatory gift and a simple transaction between me and the vision of that campaign.**

I have come to realize that true generosity includes not only a human transaction but also a spiritual transaction. When we move from a simple two-party agreement (illustrated below) to a third-party agreement that includes God, we have to release obligations that go with these gifts to God; after all, it is his money to begin with. Once we entrust the gift to God, it becomes his alone and we have to trust him to work out his purposes; the actions of the other human party should not concern us or distract us. True generosity is not a transaction or an obligatory agreement, but rather a way of life. The alternative is not frugality or "good financial sense," but a self-centered heart. So we have to fight these distractions with all we have.

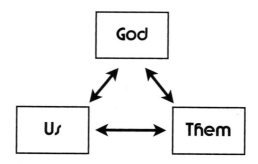

Focu/ that Defie/ Logic

In its purest form, generosity can seem indefensibly extravagant; it is irrational; it defies logic. The Gospel of Luke includes a story that demonstrates what this sort of generosity looks like.

One day Jesus, traveling across the Judean countryside, came to the house of Simon the Pharisee. Of course, it was typical for traveling teachers to be invited into another's home and to spend the evening conversing about teachings and sharing verbal traditions of the day.

On this particular evening there were a number of Pharisees gathered in Simon's home and at some point during the course of the evening an uninvited guest showed up on the scene. It was a local prostitute. No one explains exactly how she found her way into the home and we can only speculate how exactly this might have transpired.

This woman was very remorseful and full of emotion as she entered into the room full of religious men. She made her way right to Jesus, who was reclining on the floor as was customary of the time. As he reclined he was probably telling stories and discussing relevant topics. In the midst of this moment, she made her way straight for the feet of Jesus. It states clearly in the text that this woman "lived a sinful life" and we have to assume that the weight of her sin and life choices were more than she could handle any longer.

A stunned Simon watched as the woman engaged in some very specific actions. She let down her hair, kissed Jesus' feet, poured perfume on him, and began to weep uncontrollably as she knelt behind him at his feet.

This scene was obviously a little surprising to them, and perhaps profound to us, but the central action of the story is the pouring of the perfume. Alabaster perfume, as it was called, was an expensive scent of the time. It was valued at about a years' worth of day labor, which made it extremely valuable. We have to draw the necessary conclusion that this perfume was purchased with income earned from her current choice of occupation. And in symbolic fashion this woman essentially poured out her life at Jesus' feet.

While Simon was watching this scene he began pondering to himself. His thought process, not known by any spectator in the room, was clearly heard by Jesus. It says in the text that Simon thought to himself, "If this man were a prophet, he would know who is touching him and what kind of woman she is—that she is a sinner."[30] Of course, Jesus was well aware of what kind of woman she was. In response to Simon's unspoken outrage, Jesus told him a story about a moneylender.

> *"Two people owed money to a certain moneylender. One owed him five hundred denarii, and the other fifty. Neither of them had the money to pay him back, so he forgave the debts of both."[31]*

Jesus followed his story with a driving question: "Now which of them will love him more?".[32]

I am sure it wasn't long before Simon realized that this little story was really about him, his lack of generosity, and his own religious distraction.

> *Simon replied, "I suppose the one who had the bigger debt forgiven." "You have judged correctly," Jesus said.[33]*

Now he had ensnared Simon with his own answer. At this point Jesus began to point out the obvious contrast between the sinful woman and Simon. He turned to draw reference to her generosity and pointed out the fact that she was taking part in some basic actions that were standard customs of the day.

> *"Do you see this woman? I came into your house. You did not give me any water for my feet, but she wet my feet with her tears and wiped them with her hair. You did not give me a [greeting], but this woman, from the time I entered, has not stopped kissing my feet. You did not put oil on my head, but she has poured perfume on my feet."[34]*

This is a pretty brash chastisement. We can only guess the tone, but I would assume the statement itself would have stung a little.

---

[30] Luke 7:39.
[31] Luke 7:41-42.
[32] Luke 7: 42.
[33] Luke 7:43.
[34] Luke 7:44-46.

Jesus was not about to let Simon or anyone else in the house steal this beautiful moment of generosity from the woman. This woman had brought symbolically all her identity and laid it at the feet of Jesus. What she was seeking was new life, a fresh start, and forgiveness. And in this incredible moment of chastisement, Jesus turned back to the woman in reference to her generous act and open heart and said, "Your sins are forgiven."[35]

In this moment the woman's heart takes center stage in the story. Her act of generosity was extravagant and deserving of extravagant grace. The pouring of that Alabaster perfume was symbolic to her of laying down all her life; therefore Jesus would offer her forgiveness only found in the laying down of all his life.

In a very similar account in the Gospel of Matthew, this same story has an unusual nuance. It says that when the followers saw this, they were indignant. "Why this waste" they asked. "this perfume could have been sold at a high price and the money given to the poor. "[36] This one statement creates an unusual tension that I have always wanted to resolve. That tension between what is totally rational and that which is totally irrational. Simply put, **sometimes there are moments in which generosity defies human logic.**

Obviously the responsible thing to do in this situation would have been to sell this perfume and give the money to the poor. In fact the potential positive impact of this exchange could have cared for an impoverished person for a year, or an entire family for months. But this was a reality that the woman did not even consider. Her mind did not evaluate the situation or consider which choice would be best —her heart simply acted.

As much as I would like to be wise, sharp, and cunning with my money and time, there will be moments when pure acts of generosity will look irrational and unwise to outsiders. I know that wisdom should be used in all decisions, but I wonder if there is a

---

[35] Luke 7:48.
[36] Matthew 26:8-9.

point at which human wisdom should be set aside. And I am beginning to believe there is. And it is this kind of irrational generosity that teaches us to focus on the stuff that really matters. For the woman, the only thing that really mattered was forgiveness and the departure of an old way of life. This was far more valuable to her than anything else in the moment, and Jesus clearly praised her decision. She was a person who had been forgiven much, not little.

In reflecting on Simon's thoughts, and even the Pharisees' actions, what they had wrong in the moment was focus. Their focus on logic, philosophy, and the theological discourse of the moment led them away from what really mattered. Interestingly enough, only the woman truly recognized who was in the room. What she saw in Jesus was God in the flesh. What everyone else saw was simply a traveling teacher or at best a prophet, but we know for sure they did not see God. It was her focus on Jesus' divinity that created the generous response that seemed to defy logic. Human reason said, "Sell it and give to the poor." Spiritual reason said, "I have no choice but to do what might appear humanly irrational because a relationship with God is spiritually super-rational."

In my daily life there is a part of me that wants to wisely manage the time and money of my life and there is the other part that says to leave conventional wisdom behind and just be generous. Although I am a big proponent of planning, preparing, and being wise with what God blesses me with, I find that there are times God asks us to do the seemingly irrational. In this story we see one of those moments, and these moments are rare. Sometimes we will be so focused on Christ that generosity will defy logic, and human reason will take a back seat to spiritual reason.

The Complexity of Spouses

The percentage of us who are married has additional challenges that intertwine the decisions we make. We primarily discover these challenges when making complicated financial decisions. In the complexity of these moments, we will discover differing opinions that raise awareness of deep philosophical differences we each may have that the other may be surprised about. It is in these moments that heated discussions ensue. So I thought it would be appropriate to share a moment I navigated poorly in my own marriage.

So in about our fifth year of our marriage we moved into a new, larger home. Our family was growing and we would soon become a family of four—and eventually a family of five. This new home was exciting—but the lawn-care was daunting. Our old town home had literally a small patch of yard, and now we were moving to a property with about an acre of grass.

If there is one thing I hate about home ownership it is mowing the yard. I never feel less like a man than when I mow the grass. I feel like it is suburban manhood at its basest. As I am mowing the yard, my thoughts quickly drift to times when men used to conquer lands, defeat enemies, and kill their prey. And what do I get to do? I get to mow the yard. What a sappy case of suburban manhood.

In my deep hatred for the task, I especially hated mowing *this* yard. One full acre of misery. It was a two-hour task, not including trimming—a complete waste of a Saturday morning. I would have happily paid someone to do it, but we just didn't have the cash. So for that entire first summer, I dreaded Saturday morning.

As winter came and left, I began dreaming of getting a riding lawnmower, but I knew that convincing my wife that "we" needed one was not going to be an easy task. So a long-range plan was needed. I figured if she shared in my misery she would understand, so there were a couple of Saturdays where I had her mow the yard. But she proclaimed the task "good exercise." I had to change tactics.

Nothing says manhood better than complaining right? Well, I complained about everything that involved mowing. The heat. The size of our mower. The wasted Saturdays that I could have been spending with her and the kids. The edging. And finally she grew a little tired of the squeaky wheel.

One Saturday we headed out to two large retailers and took a look at riding mowers. It was awesome. I remember this day vividly. There were big ones and small ones. Ones with cup holders and others with umbrellas. Ones with attachments for the rear and others with attachments for the front. I was loving it, but the prices were steep. We chose to think it over, but I felt like she was coming along.

I had a rider mower on my mind and I couldn't get it out; it was a perfect example of the first stage of greed. Throughout the next three weeks I constantly looked online at the options and deals. I surfed the websites of just about every mower manufacturer. I began to narrow my options until I finally found the one I wanted. But there was a problem: I had not been discussing much of this with my wife. She was unaware of the extent of my private Internet musings, though I did print off the occasional ad for her.

One Saturday while she and the kids went out shopping I went out and mowed the lawn. It was a hot summer day in the mid-90s and it was painful. I was absolutely miserable. I sang the tune "Chain Gang" the entire time. Tired, hot, sweaty, and dirty, I headed in to take a shower, and immediately upon finishing I went online again. Still frustrated, I jumped on John Deere's website and was looking over their lawn tractors again. I found the one I had my sights on and clicked on it and carefully looked over the options.

I had been here many times before but this time was a little different. (Funny—many guys struggle with Internet pornography, but me, I was hooked on lawn tractors.) This time I took my browsing a step further; I wanted to see how much it would cost for delivery and tax. So I clicked through the purchase process and filled in my delivery address and credit card information. With tax and delivery it was about $1,000. But what I did next I will never forget for the rest of my life. I pushed the purchase button. With that one click, I thought I reclaimed my manhood, but I was wrong.

My wife came home about an hour later. I was planning to man-up and tell her, but then I quickly learned her shopping experience with the kids was about as frustrating as my lawn mowing experience; in situations like this I have found that timing is everything. So I held onto my secret for about two days.

On the third day, mid-morning, while I was at work, a crate mysteriously appeared in the middle of the driveway. I was not home, but my wife was. And, oh boy, this was not my finest hour as a husband. I got the phone call at work, and Christina was upset. And she was right for being upset; that was $1,000 we did not have. The following week brought a cycle of heated words, all deserved; I can safely say I paid the price for that lawnmower. It was not fun then, but, ten years later, we can laugh about it now.

This situation is indicative of the complexity of the spousal relationship. It is a perfect example of two people who are just not on the same page with each other. Spouses often have differing perspectives on spending and generosity; these ideological conflicts can **distract us from the generous life**.

The goal of becoming God-focused with your time and money becomes much more complicated when a second party has input into your schedule and expenditures. I know a number of couples whose spouses are just at differing levels of appreciation for the value of generosity; one feels stymied and one feels pressured. Surely Satan loves and encourages discord such as this, and we should not resign ourselves to it. This complexity is not easy to navigate, but by having focused discussions and making decisions together, we can find the oneness that God desires from us as a couple.

Fighting Distractions

The only way to fight for focus is to fight off our self-centeredness. This is really the bottom line for dealing with the distractions in our spiritual life and the bottom line for living in the tension between fear and greed. We have to be willing to die daily to self and its distractions. Given the chance, they will subtly draw us away from God. Selfish desires might begin with rationalization and leak in slowly, while other times it will catch us off guard with a full-frontal attack.

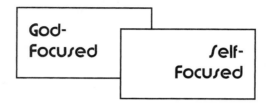

God-
Focused

Self-
Focused

John Wesley, famed 16th-century preacher and theologian, was a man who understood this battle for focus in relationship to finances. Wesley grew up in poverty, his father's preaching income unable to sufficiently support a family of fourteen. He did decide to follow his father's life path of ministry, but lived with a relentless drive to not live in poverty like his father. Instead of following his father's path into a local church, he taught at Oxford University in the early years of his ministry, and of course this situation dictated that his financial income was more substantial than that of a local pastor.

Wesley, single throughout his life, found it very easy to live a moderate lifestyle on his financial income of 30 pounds a year. His records show that in his first year at this income level, his living expenses were around 28 pounds, leaving him with two pounds to give away. The following year his income doubled, but he continued to live on 28 pounds and chose to give the other 32 pounds away. In the third year, his income increased by 30 pounds; his giving increased by the same amount. The same thing happened in year four, at which point he was giving away 92 pounds. This pattern continued until the end of his life. In some of the later years of his life he had one of the highest earned incomes in England, but his standard of living had never increased. In some of his best financial years, he was taking in over 1,400 pounds a year, yet he continued to live on simply 28 to 30 pounds a year. That's 1,370 pounds per year to the needy.

This story is staggering. Honestly, it is hard to conceive what Wesley did. He was an amazing teacher, but the story he taught about generosity was his greatest lesson. It was simply the life he lived and the generous path he chose. His choice in this matter brought him under the scrutiny of the English government, which found his actions suspicious. And others, I am sure, thought his choice to be a little extreme. But a quote from the late years of his life gives us insight into his stern beliefs in the area of generosity. **"[When I die] if I leave behind me ten pounds...you and all mankind [may] bear witness against me, that I have lived and died a thief and a robber."**[37] And at the end of his life he had no savings, no extra left over, and he had never had more than a few pounds in his possession at any one time. In other words, money had gone out as quickly as it had come in, and he had not spent it on his own wants but on the needs of others.

Living Focused

John Wesley was a man who chose to stay in the fight for focus. Wesley battled the world's beliefs, he battled with his own desires, and he chose to remain rigorously disciplined and God-centered in the area of generosity in light of all the possible distractions. But how did he get to this place of mature generosity? I think there are two answers to this question.

First, he was meticulously disciplined in living the generous and God-focused life. This is obvious from the slow, yet disciplined choices he made each year. Instead of increasing his standard of living with his cost of living, which is what you and I would be inclined to do, Wesley chose a counter-cultural approach. He chose a path of God-centeredness, not self-centeredness. And I think this same choice is ours. Generosity is a daily grind, one where we live in

---

[37] White, Charles Edward. "What Wesley Practiced and Preached About Money." *Mission Frontiers,* September/October 1994.

the middle of the distractions and tensions. We have to fight the distractions daily, and the only weapon here is dying to self and being disciplined and meticulously focused on God and his mission.

For us, being meticulously disciplined is not easy. In fact, it is a hard path, and often at first it is not done cheerfully. And, you know what? This is okay. **To begin even reluctantly is to get started, and God can take even a small amount of generosity and initiative and multiply it into something incredible.** He can take reluctant initiative and generate something beautiful for others and life changing for you. The key is to begin. Maybe you start with giving one percent of your income a year and eventually you take incremental steps toward greater discipline. I would say that setting even a modest goal such as this would give rise to generosity in your life.

So the first key to Wesley's generosity was his meticulous self-discipline. **The second key was a catalyst moment that started it all.** It was during his early years at Oxford. One day, as the story is told, Wesley had just finished paying for some pictures for his room when one of the dormitory maids came to his door. It was a cold winter day, and he noticed that she had nothing to protect her except a thin linen shirt. He reached into his pocket to give her some money to buy an appropriate winter coat but found he had too little left. Immediately, the thought struck him that God was not pleased with the way he had spent his money. He asked himself, "Will God say, 'Well done, good and faithful steward'? [You have] adorned [your] walls with the money, which might have [protected] this poor creature from the cold! O justice! O mercy! Are not these pictures the blood of this poor maid?"[38]

It was this moment that catalyzed a significant change of course for Wesley—a moment that I am sure brought to mind memories of his childhood. In fact, this one moment led to significant focus

---

[38] White, Charles Edward. "What Wesley Practiced and Preached about Money." *Mission Frontiers*, September/October 1994.

readjustment for him. To follow were many more moments just like this one. And as we know, Wesley was a man who daily walked, lived, and ate with the poor. **He choose not to distance himself from the needs of others, but allowed himself to be close to the needy all around him. And I am sure that this exposure helped him not only to start being generous but also to continue to be generous throughout his life.**

I have seen catalyst moments like this guide people toward "new births" in the areas of time and money. Often this begins with a counter-cultural experience that takes us from our current experiences and catapults us into a world that is not so materialistically wealthy. I have seen this happen in the lives of our attendees at Eagle Brook Church when people leave for Haiti, Nicaragua, or even New Orleans and see a very different way of life; these experiences often help them more than the people they are serving. Often these moments serve as a needed jolt, or catalyst, prompting a transformation of their faith and their attitudes toward time and money. And the ultimate reality is that the jolt is one that helps them to see how selfish they have been and how self-focused their choices are.

Perhaps these simple, practical steps will help you live in the tensions between fear and greed. We know our goal is to stay God-centered and mission-centered, but the hard reality is that it requires a discipline of being willing to die daily to self. And when we fail to live disciplined lives and trail off in our obedience, the best possible solution is a catalyst moment to set us straight and bring us back to living the generous life.

Discussion Questions

1. How do you typically respond to a street-side beggar? What sorts of factors influence your decision? (e.g. religious compulsion, concern for the beggar's welfare, guilt, financial problems of your own, etc.) Do you think it is possible (or even appropriate) to ignore all these distractions and simply act in generosity?

2. Have you ever pledged a donation or given a gift where you felt the gift was misused? How did this make you feel? How did you act or react to this feeling and experience?

3. When you give a gift, do you agree that it is important to completely release the obligation of how the gift is used? If so, why do you think we should practice this as a discipline?

4. Have you ever witnessed, received, or given a gift that defies logic? How did it feel to witness? How did it feel to receive? How did it feel to give?

5. John Wesley's generosity is an example of counter-cultural generosity. How extravagant would your own generosity have to become before your family would take notice? Your friends? Your neighbors? Your government?

6. How can you be meticulously disciplined in living a God-centered and generous life? How can you start being generous today even if you are reluctant? If you've already started on this journey, what was the catalyst moment that prompted you to begin?

The Prompting

"But a Samaritan, as he traveled, came where the man was; and when he saw him, he took pity on him. He went to him and bandaged his wounds, pouring on oil and wine. Then he put the man on his own donkey, brought him to an inn and took care of him. The next day he took out two denarii and gave them to the innkeeper. 'Look after him,' he said, 'and when I return, I will reimburse you for any extra expense you may have.'"

Luke 10:33-35

A Timely Prompting

Near the end of my first year of college, one of my teachers encouraged me to take a summer class on the history of Puritan churches. Even though I had been looking forward to heading home and getting away from the drudgery of school, there were a few things about this particular class that I thought were compelling. First, it was only a two-week class; that was a big win for me in that it was worth four credit hours. Second, the class was a two-week bus tour of the northeast United States, and who doesn't love experiential learning? And third, there was no homework! That detail alone sold me on the idea. The fact that the class would be a great growth experience was an afterthought.

My participation in this class required one key sacrifice: I would have to remain at school for the summer. Logistically it was going to be impossible to head back and forth between Oklahoma, where I went to school, and my home in California. But after a couple of conversations with my grandparents, I decided to stay at school for the summer, find a summer job, and enroll in the class.

I spent most of my childhood with my grandparents, Walter "Lee" and Verna Mae Baker. They were pivotal in my life in so many ways—especially in my spiritual journey. While most of my friends called their grandfathers "Grandpa," in my teen years I referred to mine as "Daddy." It goes without saying that the two of us were very close, and that my father and I were not.

I faced many challenging circumstances during my childhood. For starters, my biological parents did not follow Christ, and under that influence, neither did I. My parents divorced when I was two; my father tried to engage in a relationship with me over the following years, but this was difficult for him and I to navigate. When I was about seven years old, my mother married another man, but the marriage fell apart a few years later; this led to another divorce and the great drama that went with it. After this my mother decided not to remarry again, but she did date a variety of men. Most of these men were wealthy and had few fatherly attributes or parental desires. My mother's choices eventually led to drug addiction, loneliness, and ultimately her death. By this time my biological father was many years removed from the narrative of my life. My grandparents were really all I had.

This was a confusing environment to grow up in, and in this confusion I made some rough choices of my own. But my grandparents were an influence that I came to trust more and more as time went on. There was little stability or truth in what my mother, father, stepfather, and friends were saying, but I found my grandparents' lives to be consistent and honest. Of course, they were the only Christian influence in my life at this point. Through their prayers, consistent presence, unconditional love, and forgiveness, I had an encounter with Christ and made a decision of faith around the age of 20. In fact, it was their generous investments of time and money that led to my enrollment at that college; it was my third attempt, having already dropped out twice. But this time, at the age of 21, it was a new season and one of tremendous growth in my faith. I was beginning for the first time to find my own identity in Christ and leave my former life behind.

It was this relationship with my grandparents that made it hard not to go home over the summer. I rarely visited them due to the cost of travel, and this summer class would only extend the long gap between visits. After we talked it over, we decided it was best to stay, focus on school, and wait until the next opportunity—even if that wouldn't come until next summer.

So I stayed, found a job mowing grass on campus, and took the class. (I think this is where my hatred of mowing grass was conceived.)

I was energized about the trip all the way to the day of departure, right until I arrived at the bus stop with my bags. My first thought was that I had showed up for the wrong tour. Let's put it this way: I was the only person in my age group on the trip. Of the other forty participants, none were younger than 50, and most were women. Somehow my teacher had forgotten to mention this ever-so-small detail! I was not happy. I felt conned and betrayed. I almost grabbed my bags and went back to my apartment, but I was too ashamed to do it.

So for the next two weeks, I endured one uncomfortable moment after another. Who to sit next to? Who to talk to? Who to room with? Awkward, awkward, awkward! I struggled through all this for the entirety of the trip. But along the way, I did build some unique relationships with some people. In particular, I had the pleasure of meeting Mary, a spunky and straightforward woman in her 60s.

Mostly I sat by myself on the bus, but when I did sit with someone, it was usually Mary. She had the spirit of a 30-year-old and her no-nonsense attitude and honest perspective on life intrigued me. By the halfway point of the trip, sitting next to Mary on the bus had become something I looked forward to. Despite the generation gap, we connected and learned from each other.

The day before the trip ended, Mary and I began to share some hard stuff from each of our lives—the struggles that we each had faced as we had traveled through life. She shared some about her family and the loss of her husband and I shared about the mistakes of my life and the deep relationship I had with my grandparents. In that moment I alluded to the sacrifice I had made in coming on that trip: giving up the opportunity to go home for the summer.

Well, somewhere in this discussion, Mary insisted that I let her purchase me a round-trip ticket to my grandparents' home in California. My first response was refusal; I hadn't shared this information looking for a handout. My sacrifice had been deliberate and final. It wasn't like I was searching for a way back home. About an hour later she insisted again that I let her purchase the ticket. I refused again, with a polite "thank you." But she was just too insistent, and I could tell that I would not win in a battle of wills with this woman; in the end I graciously accepted. I did not know it at the time, but months later I would discover that Mary was a person of significant wealth—very significant wealth.

After we returned home, Mary purchased a ticket for me and had it mailed to my apartment. It was dated for four months in the future, and it was a date I would look forward to. I concealed the travel plans from my grandparents in hopes of surprising them with a visit.

Summer passed and school set in. I was back in routine and the four months flew by. Then, just two days before my unannounced trip, my grandmother called. I will never forget her words: "Son, Daddy is very sick and dying, and you need to come home now." My grandmother was in tears and very emotional as she explained that cancer had been eating at his body a while and now it had found its way into his spine; he was dying at a rapid pace.

The next two days were painful, to say the least. Packing and heading off to San Francisco International Airport was not an enjoyable experience. A friend picked me up at the airport and drove me straight to the hospital. There, in God's sovereignty, I got to spend one hour with my grandfather; my mentor; my dad.

This was probably the most memorable hour I ever spent with him. It was a painful, exciting, and curious moment. We had not seen each other for over a year. I had changed a lot spiritually and he had changed a lot physically. He mustered all the strength he could to sit up in the bed and smile at me as I entered the room. I could tell sitting up was a great and difficult task for him. He had lost a ton of weight. He was simply skin and bones; his eyes were sunken in, his skin was deeply yellowed, and his body was hairless from the battle. Intravenous tubes were dangling from his body, yet in the excitement just to converse I lost sight of most of this; his spirit, after all, was still the same. During this hour, time seemed to slow down for the two of us. My grandmother left us alone, and we just sat and talked. It was such a unique combination of emotion—the excitement to catch up with each other and the sadness of the terminal moment. I shared about my spiritual growth, we discussed the future, and he inquired about my "lady life" a little. He challenged me on choices regarding my future, which was intense and surreal. Not once did we discuss his situation, as he found these other matters far more pressing. After this hour, he explained he was tired and he lay down never to talk or rise again.

I sat for another hour in the silence of the room. In the quietness, I began to talk to God. I cannot remember if it was out loud or to myself, but it was a vivid and memorable conversation for me. During this conversation with God I made **one commitment** to him and **one request** of him. My commitment to God was this: for the rest of my life I would pour into others in the way that my grandfather had poured into me. Weeks after my grandfather's death and funeral, I changed my college major from a business degree to a ministry degree, and to this day I have been doing the work God has called me to do. My request—well, that was unique. I asked God for only one thing, and it was not in any way contingent on the previous commitment. It was a standalone, non-obligatory request. My request was that God replace my grandfather with someone else to walk through life with me. Essentially I asked him to give me someone like my grandfather. And God honored my request. Two weeks after the funeral, I went back to school and met a young transfer student from Sioux Falls, South Dakota, named Christina Brannum. We fell in love, got married, and to this day I view her as God's answer to that very specific prayer.

Interestingly enough, all this started with a woman named Mary. Mary and I didn't talk much after this trip, but **her well-timed generosity,** even though seemingly insignificant at the time, became significant in my life later. **Her willingness to be prompted to be** generous led to one of the most significant moments of my whole life. Her act of generosity gave me the opportunity to go home and be with my grandparents, to enjoy the last hour of my grandfather's life, to make a significant career change, and it led me into the most significant relationship two people can share—**all this started with a prompting**. I am so thankful that Mary's heart was open to the prompting **because it changed my life forever**.

When opportunity presents itself, we have to be ready to respond with gifts of our time or money—or both. The reality is that we have these opportunities all the time, but we either fail to understand that we are supposed to act or we find ourselves unprepared to respond, or unwilling. So how do we prepare for these promptings?

A Generous Prayer

Here is a simple suggestion that anyone can do—pray. And there are two types of prayers we can pray.

First, talk with God, or pray, before you spend any amount of money. Generosity is not simply a transaction between two people; it is **a way of life that begins with a conversation with God**. This conversation is all about us being willing to allow God, the master of all resources, to show us how we should manage and distribute these goods. And it is futile to try to just spend it without his clear direction and approval.

In my relationship with my wife **we have a clear policy of conversing**—dating back to the lawn tractor incident—about any matter of spending before we do it. Now, this does not apply to every little expense, like an occasional coffee, but it does apply to most anything above $30. We call it our $30 Policy.

In our first years of marriage, before this policy was in place, our lack of communication caused lots of problems. I would definitely say I was very selfish with my money in those first few years. Rarely did I consult with Christina; I was the one earning the money, after all, so it was my money—the operative word here being "my." As you can see, my selfishness was just oozing out of my pores during the early years of our marriage.

Over time I came to realize that even though I was the only one earning the household income, it was not "my money"—it was "our money." Together we had to manage what we had been given by God, and open discussions were an important deterrent against each of our own self-centered tendencies. This **$30 Policy** has really helped to guide our marriage to new frontiers and ensure that our own self-centered tendencies are kept in check. When I am held accountable to my wife and discuss spending opportunities before I make the purchase, I am much likelier to make wise and godly financial decisions.

The reason I have conversations with my wife about money are exactly the same reasons we should have conversations with God about money. Here are three good reasons why we should talk to God about these matters. **First, we pray with God because He loves it when we spend time with him.** I am convinced that God loves it when we "spend time" with him, and that is simply what prayer is—time with God. I would bet if you asked any Christian who is actively and daily involved in the discipline of prayer to describe the chief benefit of this time, he or she would not list God's answers to all these prayers. You know what I bet such a person would say? That the chief benefit of praying to God is the opportunity to spend time with him. And God loves it when we take one of the most important resources we have—time—and use it in talking to him.

Second, we pray with God because it his money. We have to always keep in mind that we are the manager and God is the owner; failing to remember this can lead to numerous bad decisions. Prayer is a place where we can be reminded of this arrangement with God. And prayer is our opportunity to get God's input on how we intend to use the resources he has given us. When we bypass these conversations, we damage our relationship with God. This is exactly what I did in my relationship with my wife in the episode with the lawn tractor.

Third, we pray with God because we have selfish tendencies. Usually these discussions help us to see what we need to do regardless of what we want to do.

So we need to have intimacy with God, to respect him, and to be accountable to him. We resolve all three of these needs during simple conversations with him. Praying creates accountability with God in matters where our heart can easily lead us away from making great decisions. It is never a good decision to attempt to live a godly life without consulting God.

I think a great behavior for us all would be to enforce a **$30 Policy with God** on spending. If we could just take a few minutes before spending any amount above $30, God might reveal some selfish or selfless tendency in our own heart and guide us toward living a more honoring and disciplined life with our money and time.

Obviously the most important time to pray is when we have a large financial opportunity in the very near future, especially if it relates to something we really want. Simple prayer has pulled me away from many large financial expenditures. **Money has a strong magnetic pull on our own selfish nature; prayer is the place where God keeps our emotions balanced and our centeredness on track**. Usually even a short prayer will reveal my heart's true intentions, and the more I want something, the more I need to be praying about it—regardless of how hard it might be to pray.

Second, **pray for generosity opportunities.** We have to not only converse with God about how we spend, but also ask for opportunities to be generous. Now, the surprising part about a generosity prayer is that God will almost immediately give us the opportunity to know what to do. You have to be prepared when you pray this type of prayer because answers will come quickly in most cases. I have always wondered why God is so quick to answer this type of prayer. Seriously, the speed of God's response is astounding. Just try it.

I have one conclusion on this matter. I think God gets so excited that we are not praying our usual safe and selfish prayers that he just can't wait to respond to this new, unusual, and adventurous request.

So start conversing with God; even take a moment now, and he will take you on the most amazing journey of your life.

Generosity Sightings

Even though it all begins with prayer, we have to face the reality that promptings are around us all the time. When I lift my head and open my eyes, I quickly come to realize that my needs are not the only ones to be seen. Often **there are people all around us who need God and the resources he has left under our care**, but we rarely see them.

Along with a generosity prayer, there are two simple actions we all can do, regardless of age, to engage these promptings. Following are two low-tech and high-contact activities that we have to utilize in our fast-paced society.

First, take time to look people right in the eyes. Try this for one full day. I call it the **One-Day Test**. Make eye contact with your waiter. Make eye contact with your spouse. Make eye contact with each customer. Make eye contact with your neighbor. Make eye contact with your children. Just for a few seconds, take the time. It is not a stare; it is a look of love.

In the story about the rich young man in the Gospel of Mark, it says Jesus did something very unique—it is a detail I have missed numerous times.

The story takes place during Jesus' travels throughout the Judean countryside. He entered a village and was confronted by crowds of people. These people had come to him seeking healing, hope, and change. Crowds of broken, hurting, terminal, and destitute people were flocking to Jesus. But from within the scene arose a young man with no physical needs, no monetary needs, and seemingly no religious needs—yet he had come to seek something from Jesus. The man who surfaced from the crowd was the richest man in town. He was wealthy, sharp, educated, young, and blessed in every worldly way. I am sure everyone in the crowd had the same question: "What does this man need of Jesus? He has everything."

The text says he ran up to Jesus and fell on his knees before him. He brought a deep and theologically significant question.

> *"Good teacher," he asked, "what must I do to inherit eternal life?"*[39]

Great question. Honestly I would probably have asked a very similar question if this was me, especially if I had a degree of uncertainty about what I believed. I personally believe his request was well intentioned and deeply honest. And Jesus replied to his inquiry.

> *"Why do you call me good?" Jesus answered. "No one is good—except God alone. You know the commandments: You shall not murder, you shall not commit adultery, you shall not steal, you shall not give false testimony, you shall not defraud, honor your father and mother."*[40]

This response from Jesus would not have taken anyone there by surprise. Every Jew, including this young man, had memorized these commandments from the Law and was able to repeat them at will. This young man was no different. Notice his response: "'Teacher,' he declared, 'all these I have kept since I was a boy.'"[41]

In concluding this moment, Jesus requested just one more thing from him. One really big thing.

---

[39] Mark 10:17.
[40] Mark 10:18-19.
[41] Mark 10:20.

"One thing you lack," [Jesus] said. "Go, sell everything you have and give to the poor, and you will have treasure in heaven. Then come, follow me."
At this the man's face fell. He went away sad, because he had great wealth.[42]

What Jesus was asking of him was simultaneously deep generosity and deep commitment to God's mission; both of these are tied so tightly together. But the single sentence that gives me pause is the one that appears right in the middle of the narrative. It comes right after the young man's declaration, "All these I have kept since I was a boy," and right before Jesus utters the words, "One thing you lack." The words are as follows:

"Jesus looked at him and loved him."[43]

I have always wondered what Jesus' face looked like in this moment. My assumption is that there was this long pause right before he spoke the words, "One thing you lack." I also want to assume that the place and the surroundings were silent. That everyone leaned in for the deep truth that would fall from Christ's lips—for that one thing, that one all-encompassing truth, that Holy Grail. But Jesus just looked. He looked and he loved.

Sometimes this is all that is needed—just a look. People around us are hurting and waiting for someone to be generous, and I wonder if Jesus saw them simply because he looked.

I think it would be shocking to you to take the **One-Day Test** and make eye contact with every person you come in contact with; there is a story in every person's eyes that will speak truth about their own hurts, pains, and disappointments, and their joys, hopes, and delights.

---

[42] Mark 10:21-22.
[43] Mark 10:21a.

Just as important, take a separate day just to listen to people. The One-Day Test does not end with simply looking, but includes the ability to listen. Again, it is simple; just ask questions of people you see everyday. Get to know them on another level. Inquire about their family, life, friends, likes, strengths, leadership, and future.

Just a short while back, an employee stepped into my office. We had set up a one-hour meeting that we forgot to cancel. But even though there was no business to attend to, we met anyway. Most days, both of our calendars are jam-packed with stuff and we joke that there are many days we barely have time to even use the restroom. This has actually become a little bit of a sarcastic truism about our work life. Between our busyness and the fact that the two of us do not work directly with each other, we had never managed to get to know each other; we decided to take advantage of the open hour to do just that. We discussed family, our past, and our lives before Christ and after. We discussed kids, sports, and our own little musings. After a while we discussed work, our staff, and our own leadership challenges. And I have to say it was one of the best hours I have had in a long time. At the end of the hour, we both smiled at how enjoyable that was, and went about the rest of that day. Isn't it interesting how enjoyable it can be to simply listen? And I think God wants us to do much more of this than we do.

I am never going to become a generous person if I am not aware of the needs of people around me, so I must both look and listen to catch sight of the opportunities that God wants to give me. This One-Day Test helps me to become more aware of my surroundings and helps to provide the needed boost to my promptings. It is a discipline we have to engage in if we are going to become obedient and generous people.

Discussion Questions

1. Have you ever been prompted to give time or money for an unexplainable reason? Describe the moment and the recipient.

2. It is relatively common to pray before committing to a large expense (like the purchase of a new home), but have you ever prayed before making a comparatively smaller purchase? What prompted you to pray?

3. If married, do you feel like you and your spouse have similar attitudes toward finances? Toward generosity? How do you try to align yourselves in these areas? Have you ever instituted something similar to a $30 policy?

4. Have you ever prayed for an opportunity to be generous? If yes, how did God respond? If no, why do you find this prayer intimidating?

5. Challenge yourself to take the One-Day Test of either intentional eye-contact or intentional listening. At the end of the day, consider these questions: Did you learn anything surprising from someone you know well? Did you have any rewarding contact with a stranger?

The Ultimate Act

"Greater love has no one than this: to lay down one's life for one's friends."

John 15:13

A Story of Sacrifice

There would be no better way to close off a discussion on generosity than to present the ultimate act of generosity this world has ever known: the sacrifice of Christ's life. And since I could not tell it more beautifully, listen to John's discourse on the final moments of his life.

> *Finally Pilate handed him over to them to be crucified. So the soldiers took charge of Jesus. Carrying his own cross, he went out to the place of the Skull (which in Aramaic is called Golgotha). There they crucified him, and with him two others—one on each side and Jesus in the middle.*
>
> *Pilate had a notice prepared and fastened to the cross. It read: JESUS OF NAZARETH, THE KING OF THE JEWS. Many of the Jews read this sign, for the place where Jesus was crucified was near the city, and the sign was written in Aramaic, Latin and Greek.*
>
> *Later, knowing that everything had now been finished, and so that Scripture would be fulfilled, Jesus said, "I am thirsty." A jar of wine vinegar was there, so they soaked a sponge in it, put the sponge on a stalk of the hyssop plant, and lifted it to Jesus' lips. When he had received the drink, Jesus said, "It is finished." With that, he bowed his head and gave up his spirit.*[44]

The prophet Isaiah says it this way, hundreds of years before Jesus' crucifixion:

> *He grew up before him like a tender shoot, and like a root out of dry ground. He had no beauty or majesty to attract us to him, nothing in his appearance that we should desire him. He was despised and rejected by mankind, a man of suffering, and familiar with pain. Like one from whom people hide their faces he was despised, and we held him in low esteem.*

---

[44] John 19:16-20, 28-30.

Surely he took up our pain and bore our suffering, yet we considered him punished by God, stricken by him, and afflicted. But he was pierced for our transgressions, he was crushed for our iniquities; the punishment that brought us peace was on him, and by his wounds we are healed. We all, like sheep, have gone astray, each of us has turned to our own way; and the Lord has laid on him the iniquity of us all.

He was oppressed and afflicted, yet he did not open his mouth; he was led like a lamb to the slaughter, and as a sheep before its shearers is silent, so he did not open his mouth. By oppression and judgment he was taken away. Yet who of his generation protested? For he was cut off from the land of the living; for the transgression of my people he was punished. He was assigned a grave with the wicked, and with the rich in his death, though he had done no violence, nor was any deceit in his mouth.

Yet it was the Lord's will to crush him and cause him to suffer, and though the Lord makes his life an offering for sin, he will see his offspring and prolong his days, and the will of the Lord will prosper in his hand. After he has suffered, he will see the light of life and be satisfied; by his knowledge my righteous servant will justify many, and he will bear their iniquities. Therefore I will give him a portion among the great, and he will divide the spoils with the strong, because he poured out his life unto death, and was numbered with the transgressors. For he bore the sin of many, and made intercession for the transgressors.[45]

We only hear a few spoken words in these final hours of Christ's life. The rest of it was a pure act of generosity. Jesus held complete power and authority over all creation. Throughout his short life he proved his power over time and space, over human DNA, and over the elements of the earth. He read the minds of people and he dazzled them with his own intellect. His wisdom was spectacular, and his compassion like none other. And his greatest act was one of complete generosity for all people. One generous act for all time. Not just an act of generosity for the present, but one that reached into the past and into the future. This one act became the greatest story ever told. In every generation since Christ, people have written

---

[45] Isaiah 53.

plays, painted pictures, filmed movies, and composed songs in an attempt to capture this act of generosity, this story of all stories.

And this generous act was for you and me.

I wonder if we just forget. I wonder if our root problem with living generously is as simple as this: we have forgotten how generous God has been to us. And his desire for each of us is that we would live out the generosity he has modeled for us. Though we may not offer the literal sacrifice of our life for another, we can definitely offer the time and money under our care.

But these final days of Christ's life demonstrate that time and money are not the only objects we must submit in living the generous life. According to Jesus' model, the ultimate focus of generosity is the sum of all actions in our life. Generosity involves the willingness of the heart to act in love toward God's purposes with our whole being from the moment we make an initial confession of Christ as Lord.

This spirit of generosity was perfectly modeled by Christ, but his example is not the only one Scripture offers us, nor the first. In Abraham we see a man willing to be generous with his most prized blessing: his son of promise and future. In Nehemiah we see a man willing to sacrifice his life and reputation as cupbearer to the king in service to his Jewish brothers and the city of Jerusalem. In Daniel we see a man willing to sacrifice his life for his integrity; he is generously faithful to God at all cost, regardless of the impeding fate of the lion's den. Stories like these are never-ending in the Old Testament, and all the subjects share one trait in common: their deep generosity, which extends beyond time and money. They do not cling to their visions, to their families, or to their future plans; they withhold nothing, offering their very lives.

But how do these men and women live such generous lives? It is the act of Christ's sacrifice that empowers them and us to become generous. This one act for all time enables us to know generosity and become generous to others. The letter to the Ephesians says that we were formerly living in an old life corrupted by evil desires—or corrupted by selfishness that lacked the ability to be generous—yet now, empowered by the personal indwelling of the Holy Spirit, we are sealed with the power to live a new life, one of generosity. We are empowered as Christ's followers with the power to be conduits of his generosity. As the author of Ephesians explains, we are called to be generous conduits of Christ's grace, wisdom, understanding, forgiveness, truth, kindness, mercy, and ultimately the endless love of God. We are not called to be selfish with these riches he lavished on us, but to generously lavish on others the same riches he has shared with us. When we hold back from sharing these riches with others, we actually diminish the power of God, damming up his streams of grace and mercy.

The reality is that we all struggle to live daily in the place where God can fully use us. I assume you, like me, struggle daily to be generous with your life and live in the spectrum between selfishness and selflessness. I know I do. And when all else fails to revive the stream of my generosity, the greatest practice for me is reflecting on the moment I first made a commitment to Christ as Lord. It was in this moment that I first felt the heavens open to me as God lavished his grace, mercy, and forgiveness upon me in my hopeless state. The reality I have faced in my own life is that without this moment I would not be the man I am today. I am imperfect—yes—but growing, learning, and becoming like Christ in his generosity a little more every day. The last twenty years of my spiritual journey have been amazing, and I generously pray for you the same. Live the generous life!

Discussion Questions

1. Name a movie, play, painting, or song that attempts to portray the sacrifice of Jesus's death: What attributes are emphasized in this art? What attributes does this art fail to capture in comparing this with Jesus vast generosity?

2. Jesus was the ultimate model of sacrifice, but can you think of other examples in the Old and New Testament of people who lived the generous life? Of your list which character rises to the top of the list as the best representation of Christ's generosity?

3. Think of someone in your own life who you consider to be generous. Which of their sacrifices has particularly caught your attention?

4. The generous life requires a willingness to fully surrender; which object or aspect of your life do you find most difficult to surrender to Christ?

5. God, in his generosity, offers us the riches of his grace, mercy, forgiveness, and love. In turn, we are supposed to be vehicles through which God distributes these riches to others. How has God blessed you in the last week or month? Can you identify the person(s) he has used to distribute this blessing? Consider for a moment whether these riches are meant for you alone. If not, can you identify someone in need of your surplus?

Appendix:

Generosity for Leaders

"I am astonished that you are so quickly deserting the one who called you to live in the grace of Christ and are turning to a different gospel—which is really no gospel at all. Evidently some people are throwing you into confusion and are trying to pervert the gospel of Christ. But even if we or an angel from heaven should preach a gospel other than the one we preached to you, let them be under God's curse! As we have already said, so now I say again: If anybody is preaching to you a gospel other than what you accepted, let them be under God's curse!"

Galatians 1:6-9

"Not many of you should become teachers, my fellow believers, because you know that we who teach will be judged more strictly."

James 3:1

I figured going without a short chapter for pastors, teachers, and fundraisers might be amiss. Over the last fifteen years of my ministry career, I have seen some interesting tactics used in the area of fundraising. Some of these tactics have made me feel very uncomfortable. I often struggle in the moment to articulate why these tactics bother me so much, but the bottom line is that they do not feel like the gospel I read. And when these tactics don't match up with the gospel, then I become concerned about what we are teaching the people who are following our lead.

So the following list is for my colleagues who are pastors, teachers, fundraisers, leaders, ministers, elders, deacons, directors, board members, and advisors. When we are trying to raise funds, engage in expansion, build buildings, and gather money from potential donors, we must remember we are teaching our people what we deeply believe about money. Some of these people are going to be young in their faith, and how we ask for donations, partnership, or funding matters because we will be teaching them inadvertently about what God believes about money. We are directing people's lives and, as Paul says in Galatians 1:6-9, we will be held accountable for the gospel we teach or fail to teach.

If you are a leader of any kind who is asking for money or time from others, remember that how you engage in this task is important. When you ask for funds, you are not simply fostering a business partnership. It is something far more. It is an opportunity to teach, to share the true gospel, to extend vision, and to be in ministry partnership with those who are not vocationally involved with ministry. These people we invite to our financial vision will be our friends, family members, school colleagues, or recipients of the ministry we do.

The following are insights I have gleaned from my ministry career. I think our members, regular attenders, and first-time guests would support much of what you will read here.

First, never lose sight of generosity. You will be tempted along the way to steer away from teaching people how to live generously. The temptation to ask people to simply give is strong, especially in seasons when there is great need. We have to remember that asking people to give to a need is simply a quick fix and will often distract from generous living. The act of reducing our teaching to mere giving tactics can become increasingly self-serving for our organizations, and others will notice this immediately. Intuitively people will know generosity when they see it. Remember to keep the gospel of generosity within your sights at all times—especially in seasons of economic need.

Second, teach openhandedness toward local and global ministries. By teaching your attenders and members how to become generous with their time and money toward others, you will guide their hearts toward managing their own resources well. But it requires mature and secure leadership to teach this type of openhandedness and to ignore the concern that members and attenders might funnel resources away from the local church and into other ministries. Let's call this concern what it actually is: self-serving fear and deep insecurity in God's providence. I know those are strong words, but this is the truth about this concern. This fear, as we have already discussed, never leads to God-honoring decisions, and for us it never leads to God-honoring leadership. We as leaders should be able to encourage our attenders and members to disperse their resources generously to the local church and beyond—even at a slight cost to our church's bottom line. The fear that leads to this selfish concern is something we have to release to God. We must not project this fear and selfishness on our attenders because once this pattern is learned, it is not easily unlearned. And once this fearful and selfish posture is learned, it will become a vicious disease to our church or organization.

Third, teach first steps, but don't focus on the tithe. To focus only on the tithe is to lose focus on the ultimate mission and to exchange a generous way of life for a simple giving action. The goal is not to focus on minimums, or simply 10%, but to focus on maximums, or the 100% that God desires from us all. Don't ask people simply to give, but rather teach the gospel of generosity. We can start people with a percentage, but we have to ensure that people understand that this is only a place to begin. And this is the beauty of Acts chapter four:

> *All the believers were one in heart and mind. No one claimed that any of their possessions was their own, but they shared everything they had. With great power the apostles continued to testify to the resurrection of the Lord Jesus. And God's grace was so powerfully at work in them all that there were no needy persons among them. For from time to time those who owned land or houses sold them, brought the money from the sales and put it at the apostles' feet, and it was distributed to anyone who had need. Joseph, a Levite from Cyprus, whom the apostles called Barnabas (which means "son of encouragement"), sold a field he owned and brought the money and put it at the apostles' feet.*[46]

Fourth, don't collude with third parties. Third-party collusion is often a poorly motivated partnership. This third party in fundraising is often a person of great financial means. I have never seen collusion with a third party work out well unless his or her heart's motivation is very well placed; unfortunately, it is very difficult to evaluate someone's heart. Often this third party has a particular agenda for his or her gift and is only giving under the guise of generosity; even though we would really like to obtain the gift, we

---

[46] Acts 4:32-36.

know this decision may lead to others that would not honor God. I personally believe collusion with third parties can lead to future foolish decisions. (I am referring specifically to human third parties; as I explained in the chapter on distractions, God is an appropriate and necessary third party in all our relationships.)

I need to include here a warning regarding vision-funding campaigns. When we cast vision for a campaign in a volatile or changing economic climate, we are in danger of not being able to deliver on a promise to our members and attenders. I would call this collusion, just a different form. It is collusion with an idea or an ideal. Colluding in this way can be a risky gamble. I suggest casting vision broadly; make mention of your church's needs only if they can be accomplished with certainty within a specific amount of time. We need to always keep in mind that churches are living organisms, and economic climates are organic as well. They don't always respond exactly like we want or like we plan. We should enter larger capital campaigns with a lot of prayer these days, and not make these large-scale decisions independently of others.

Fifth, teach ownership at every level from small children to older adults. Ensure that all audiences are learning the heart of generosity. Even once we learn the concepts of generosity, it can take years to step out in faith and live the generous life. We all know that it is our older members who are faithful donors and financial partners in the mission, but teaching generosity at every level will benefit you and many others down the road. One of your greatest wins could be teaching generosity to the children in your church. These children are still very pliable in their giving practices, and honestly they often understand the impulse of generosity better than adults who have been subjected to years of selfish behaviors. And when we teach our children, we also teach their parents how to live generously.

Sixth, use common language. A uniform language is key to the advancement of generosity. One of the realities we faced as a church was that even though many people were often being generous, we rarely called it "generosity." We called it a mission trip, a serving opportunity, a chance to volunteer, an offering, a special contribution, a campaign contribution, and a regular giving opportunity, but we never called it just one thing! Satan loves confusion like this. I am confused just thinking about all the things we used to call it. How can we teach anything if we don't teach just one thing? We chose the language "Be Generous." Our tag line is "with your time and money." This is simple, straightforward, and easy to communicate. "Be generous with your time and money." Even kids can comprehend this.

Seventh, remember that people who give to your ministry are partners. The people who partner with you are not simply donors. They are not purely target contacts. They are not merely people of low, medium, and high capacity. They are not purely a mailing list. These people are our "partners in ministry." They are essentially doing work with us, and when we who are called to full-time vocation ministry do our work, they are in the field working with us. We cannot treat our partners like distant relatives twice-removed; we have to treat them as close partners in the mission. Partners who want to be communicated with regularly, who want to pray with us, who need to know our honest difficulties, and who want to hear our latest success. Along the way it will be easy to grow farther from our partners, but we need to grow closer. They, too, are our ministries and they would like to be treated as such and not simply a dollar sign.

Eighth, we have to remember that we are responsible to assist in the spiritual development of the people under our care. Our teaching and leadership has the power to clarify or confuse a person's understanding of generosity. And with this we must keep in mind that we have the power to uphold the credibility or destroy the credibility of Christ based on how we present these concepts. Our attenders, members, and especially our first-time guests can sniff out our lack of generosity almost immediately. When we seek gifts and not generosity, they are going to know something is out of place, so how we teach on this topic is critical.

The greatest opportunity to teach is not from the stage platform, but from the platform of our lives. People must see our own generosity pour from our lives if they are to do the same. We must be generous as pastors and leaders. This means we ourselves must give of our time and our money. As leaders we probably have awareness that not all of our staff are currently giving to our organization or church. They somehow **rationalize** why they do not, and we have already discussed what this rationalization leads to. Being on staff at a church does not exclude us from living generously. We should be giving regularly, and if we can't, we need to ask ourselves the hard question—why? If we do not live generously, people will know. People will know by how you talk about money and how you spend your time—and even if they fail to notice, God is completely aware. This may seem like a strong challenge for the end of a book on generosity, but it is time we as leaders step up our game and not just ask our attenders and members to step up theirs.

As I close, I would like to remind the leaders that we must simply lead. We have to lead God's people toward generosity because no one else is going to do it. Our attenders, members, and guests are learning exactly the opposite of generosity from the world, and they need to hear Christ's message on the topic. These challenges are many, but the journey is worth it. And I myself am still growing, thinking, and doing my best to understand these concepts at a personal level and as a church leader. Let's grow to understand together along the way.

I look forward to hearing from you.

Vince Miller – <u>vince.miller@eaglebrookchurch.com</u>